Modern Britain

An Introduction

For Christina and Tom
with love

Modern Britain

An Introduction

John Irwin

ARCHON BOOKS 1976

First published in 1976
by George Allen & Unwin Publishers Ltd., London, and in
the United States of America as an Archon book, an imprint
of The Shoe String Press, Inc., Hamden, Connecticut 06514

© George Allen & Unwin (Publishers) Ltd 1976

Library of Congress Cataloging in Publication Data

Irwin, John L   1942–
  Modern Britain.

  Bibliography: p.
  Includes index.
  1. Great Britain.   I. Title.
DA27.5.I78   941   76-21781
ISBN 0-208-01618-x

Printed in Great Britain

Preface

In writing a book like this, one of the most difficult tasks is to decide what should be put in and what should be left out. It is obviously impossible to give a fully comprehensive account of all aspects of every British institution in a book of this length, but nevertheless I hope that it will at least serve as an introduction to some of the key features of modern British life. Another problem is that Britain is not a static society. During the writing of the book many things have changed, while others are still in the course of changing. Whenever possible account has been taken of new developments and I hope that the reader is not too irritated if he finds that an institution described in the book has changed its function, been modified or, possibly, disappeared altogether. Perhaps it may serve to prove that Britain is not quite as conservative as he thought; some things do change!

I must acknowledge the assistance of many people in writing this book, a large number of them being my former students at the University of Turku and the Turku School of Economics. It was their questions and (frequently critical) comments about British institutions that first persuaded me that it should be written. I should also thank my former colleagues at both these institutions for their help and advice, in particular George Maude and Geoffrey Alcock, both of whom were good enough to read the manuscript and make helpful suggestions. Of course none of those who have assisted me bear any responsibility for what I have written – that is mine alone.

My greatest debt is to my wife, Merja, for her help, encouragement and patience, while I should also acknowledge the tolerance of my children, who (most of the time) allowed me to work in peace.

Contents

1

Introduction to Britain

The British Isles are situated off the north-west coast of Europe. At one time they were part of the European landmass, but following the last great ice age the level of the sea rose, and the land area which now forms the British Isles became separated from the rest of the continent by a stretch of water. It is true that at its narrowest point this water is only some twenty miles wide, but those twenty miles have had a great effect on the development of Britain, for the gap is not only physical, it is psychological too. Britain is at the same time part of, but separate from, Europe, and this has had far-reaching implications for the development of all aspects of life, social, political, economic and linguistic.

The fact that Britain is on the western side of the European continent meant that when trade routes went overland to the East, Britain was on the fringe of Europe, and was virtually ignored. With the discovery of the New World in the late fifteenth and early sixteenth centuries, and the development of ocean trade routes, Britain became more important. She was in a position to dominate western trade and was not slow to take advantage of this. As Britain was an island she had to depend on shipping for her contact with her neighbours, whether she wanted to trade with them or fight them. This meant that the British had to be conversant with ships and the sea. The new trade routes lay across the oceans and Britain was to build the basis of her power and wealth on her navies.

Island states have usually found that the sea can be both an advantage and a disadvantage as far as defence is concerned. Although the sea can provide a moat, it can also be a highway for invaders, and this has been so in the case of Britain. Until 1066 the North Sea and the English Channel were a wide highway, on which invaders from Germany, Scandinavia and Normandy sailed at different times. After 1066, however, the seas proved to be a moat; for since that date there has been no successful military invasion of Britain by a foreign power. This is very important for an understanding of British institutions, for it has meant that following the Norman Conquest, with its far-reaching implications for English society, foreign institutions and customs have never been forcibly imposed on the British. Thus the form of government, the legal system and many other aspects of British life have developed in a particularly British, some would say insular, way. This is not to say, of course, that Britain has been completely free of foreign influence throughout her history. However ideas, institutions and other contributions from overseas have not been introduced by an invading army or occupying force, nor have foreign customs and ways of life been forced upon the inhabitants against their will.

This freedom from invasion can be attributed to a number of factors, one of the most important being the English Channel itself. Although wider seas than the Channel have been success-fully crossed – while the British themselves have on more than one occasion invaded Europe across the Channel – the fact remains that whenever invasion has threatened, the British have managed to retain control of the waters between Britain and the continent. Another factor that should be taken into con-sideration is that Britain is not on the way to anywhere. It is true that Britain lies on the sea routes to the Americas, but by definition a sea route does not go overland. Continental indus-trialists and merchants wanting to develop their trade with the New World could easily avoid Britain by sailing round her coasts. Nor do any other countries lie on the far side of Britain, so she has never been used as a corridor through which foreign armies have marched or fought, as has been the fate of coun-tries such as Belgium, Finland and Poland. Should, however, a situation develop in the future in which the United States, or any other American country, wanted to attack Europe, it is probable that Britain would be the first country to fall. The attacker could then use British territory as a base for subse-quent operations. Indeed this has already happened, with the compliance and assistance of the British government and people. In 1944 Europe was invaded by a force that had a very large North American contingent, and an American commander.

It has already been mentioned that the British Isles lie off the north-west coast of Europe. To be more precise, the 0° meridian passes through Greenwich (slightly east of London), while latitude 50°N passes through the Lizard peninsula, in the south of England, and latitude 60°N lies across the Shetlands, off the north coast of Scotland. From the south coast to the northern-most point on the Scottish mainland is a distance of just under 600 miles (966 kilometres), while the east and west coasts are about 300 miles (483 kilometres) apart at their widest point.

Geographically the British Isles are made up of a number of islands, and there are also a number of different political components. Very often 'England' is used as a synonym for Britain, while 'Englishman' is employed as a blanket description for all the inhabitants of the British Isles. This, as any Welshman, Irishman or Scot will quickly point out, is incorrect. The United Kingdom consists of England and Wales, Scotland and Northern Ireland. The Isle of Man, in the Irish Sea, and the Channel Islands, off the coast of France (and formerly part of the Duchy of Normandy), are not part of the United Kingdom. They are Crown dependencies, with their own legislative assemblies and legal systems. The Irish Republic, Southern Ireland, is politically entirely separate from the United Kingdom, and has been so since 1922. The term Great Britain is used to describe the three countries of England, Wales and Scotland. The total land area of the United Kingdom is 93,025 square miles (240,934 sq km), made up as follows: England, 50,052 (129,634); Wales, 7,968 (20,637); Scotland, 29,799 (77,179); and Northern Ireland 5,206 (13,484). The Isle of Man has an area of 227 square miles (588 sq km) and the Channel Islands, 75 square miles (194 sq km).

England became a united kingdom in the ninth century and Wales, which had formerly been a principality, was incorporated into this kingdom in the early Middle Ages. England and Ireland were ruled by the same king by the end of the thirteenth century, but in fact much of Ireland remained completely outside English influence. Relations between England and Ireland have rarely been good, as the Irish have resented English interference with their religious and economic life, while the English have tended to regard the Irish with a mixture of indifference and superiority. England and Scotland came under one king when James VI of Scotland ascended the English throne in 1603, though the Act of Union, which abolished the Scottish Parliament, was not passed until 1707. The Scots retained their legal system, schools and local government structure. In 1800 the Irish Parliament was discontinued and Ireland, like Scotland, was ruled from Westminster. After years of bitter struggle the twenty-six counties of southern Ireland became independent in 1922, though the six northern counties, which had a Protestant majority, remained part of the United Kingdom. Northern Ireland had its own Parliament at Stormont in Belfast, but in 1972, following several years of grave unrest, this Parliament was suspended and direct rule was imposed from Westminster. In June 1973 elections were held for a new Northern Ireland Assembly with advisory powers, but this body collapsed in early 1974. In 1975 a further attempt to solve the problem of Northern Ireland was made when an elected Convention was established, but to date there is little to suggest that this body has been any more successful than its predecessors in coming up with a solution to the problems of Northern Ireland.

The whole question of Northern Ireland, which has hardly been out of the newspaper headlines in Britain since the present disturbances began in 1969, is too complex to be dealt with in this book. Suffice it to say that at the present time a solution of the problem in political terms seems remote. The British government have repeatedly stressed that they would not be willing to withdraw their forces and permit the opposing factions to find their own solution, presumably because they feel this would mean an immediate and extremely violent civil war. However there is evidence that the population of mainland Britain is growing increasingly hostile to both the 'Loyalists' (who come from the Protestant section of the community and favour maintaining the link with Britain) and the 'Republicans' (most of whom are Roman Catholics and who want Northern Ireland to join with the counties of the South in a united Irish state). Feelings against the branch of the Irish Republican Army known as the 'Provisionals' run particularly high as they and their supporters have been involved in a number of bombing incidents in English towns, some of which have resulted in loss of life.

Both Wales and Scotland have active nationalist movements, but in the main they seem to prefer working through Parliament to using violence (though both the 'Free Wales Army' and the 'Tartan Army' have been involved in bombing attacks at various times). As we shall see, both of these nationalist movements have been enjoying considerable success in recent elections.

Following the Second World War there were those who felt that the future of Britain lay with Europe. In spite of active campaigning, however, they were unable to convince the politicians who were in power (or, the evidence suggests, the people of Britain), and when the European Economic Community (the EEC) was established Britain remained outside. By the early 1960s opinions had changed, among the government of the day at least, and the United Kingdom applied for membership of the EEC. Negotiations followed, but in 1963 British entry was vetoed by President De Gaulle. The application was renewed in 1967, but very little progress was made until 1970 when detailed discussions got under way. The Treaty of Accession was signed in early 1972 and Britain formally became a member of the Community in January 1973. The terms of accession were attacked by the Labour Party (even though they had been responsible for reopening negotiations in 1967) and they announced that if they were returned to power they would 'renegotiate' the terms of entry and then hold a referendum on the question of membership. In February 1974 the Labour Party won the election and talks commenced shortly afterwards with Britain's Common Market colleagues. These talks continued until late spring 1975 and in June of that year Britain's first referendum took place. Opposing continuing membership of the EEC were many members of the Labour Party, some Conservatives, the Nationalist parties and the Trades Union Congress (the TUC); in favour were a majority of members of the Government, the Conservative leadership and most of the rank and file membership, and the majority of British industrialists and business interests. The referendum was held on 5 June; 17,378,581 votes (67·2 per cent of those cast) were in favour of Britain remaining in the EEC, 8,470,073 votes (32·8 per cent) were in favour of leaving the Community. Following the declaration of the result, many of those who had supported the anti-Common Market line announced they would accept the decision, including the TUC and most of the Labour ministers who had spoken against continued membership.

2

The System of Government in Britain

The British system of government is the product of centuries of development that has followed no precise pattern or rigid lines, but rather a course of trial and error. This has at times led to passionate disagreements and bitter feuds, and on some occasions to open conflict. As Britain has no written constitution and relies on a mixture of statute law, common law and conventions (that is practices and precepts that although not part of a legal code are nevertheless generally accepted), the system of government has remained flexible. Sometimes the system has appeared to be too flexible and different interpretations of the role of certain institutions have been possible at different periods of time. Thus one will find no exact definition of the duties and powers of the British Head of State, beyond the fact that Britain is a monarchy. In theory the monarch's powers appear to be as absolute as they were during the Middle Ages, but in practice this power is restricted in a number of ways.

The system of government that exists in Britain today can perhaps be best described as a mixed governmental system, with the monarch seeming to be, and Parliament in fact being, the senior partner. The monarchy is hereditary, and so when a king or queen dies he or she is automatically succeeded by the next in line. Membership of the House of Lords is largely hereditary too, though there are also various categories of life peers. The lower house, the House of Commons, is however elected by the British people, and thus represents, or is claimed to represent, their wishes. Over the centuries the Crown and the Lords, that is the hereditary elements of the system, have gradually lost power to the Commons, the representatives of the people.

THE MONARCHY

The British have always been ruled by a monarch, except for a brief period during the seventeenth century, and even then the royal line was restored in 1660 shortly after the death of Oliver Cromwell, the Lord Protector. Thus the present sovereign, Elizabeth II, can claim an unbroken descent dating back to the Saxon kings, while other ancestors include Charlemagne, Malcolm II of Scotland and the Emperor Barbarossa. Nevertheless the succession has not always passed peacefully to the next in line and there are claimants to the throne today who base their case on descent from the Stuarts, who were driven from power in 1688. But there is little danger that latter-day Jacobites will dethrone the Queen, as in addition to her hereditary right she reigns with the consent of Parliament, as has every monarch since William III.

Those who are opposed to the system of monarchy often start by arguing that the institution is non-democratic, as the monarch is not subject to appointment and dismissal by the people and so can become an autocrat. When it is pointed out that this could not occur in Britain because the powers of the Crown are so limited, a further objection is made: 'Why keep the monarchy if it has no function except a ceremonial one?' To answer this we must look at the Queen's duties and see what in fact her functions are.

The visitor to Britain will not have to be unduly observant to notice evidence of the omnipresence of the Queen. Coins and stamps bear a picture of the Queen's head, the post is carried by the 'Royal' Mail, the ships in the 'Royal' Navy are 'Her Majesty's Ships', while 'Her Majesty's Government' is made up of 'Her Majesty's Ministers' and official letters are sent 'On Her Majesty's Service'. The variety and number of institutions bearing the prefix 'Royal' or 'Her Majesty's' suggests that the power of the monarch is considerable. But it is obvious that the Queen is not able to supervise the activities of even a fraction of them, and it soon becomes evident that such prefixes appear as a synonym for 'State' or 'British' when used in official titles, and do not imply that the Queen is in direct control of all the things that are done in her name. This is in fact the key to the problem: all the actions of government are carried out in the Queen's name, and automatically have her approval, although she has no personal knowledge of them.

The monarch, then, is the personification of the British state. When Louis XIV said (or was reputed to say) 'L'état c'est moi', he was speaking as an absolute monarch. When the twentieth-century British citizen says that his Queen is the personification of the state, he means that she is the symbol of the state. This is the true function of the British monarch today – a symbol – and as such the Queen's functions are virtually all ceremonial. She opens Parliament, but takes no part in its deliberations and is in fact forbidden to enter the chamber of the House of Commons, as all monarchs have been since Charles I in 1641 rashly tried to arrest five Members of whom he disapproved. No Bill can become an Act, that is have the force of law, unless the monarch has approved it, but the power of veto has not been used for more than two centuries, and any attempt to block legislation by its use would precipitate a constitutional crisis of major proportions.

It is in relation to Parliament, however, that the monarch appears to retain real power, for it is the monarch who has the responsibility of choosing the Prime Minister and other government ministers. However, in practice, the Queen must choose the leader of the party which has the majority in the House of Commons. It is the electorate who decide which the largest party will be, and the members of the party who select their leader, and so the Queen's freedom of choice is extremely limited. Once a Prime Minister has been appointed it is he[1] who chooses the members of the Government, and these men and women are then presented to the Queen as 'her' ministers.

Until recently the monarch exercised more freedom of action in choosing a Prime Minister, and there have been several occasions this century when the monarch's choice was not the obvious one. In 1923 George V asked Stanley Baldwin to form a government in succession to Bonar Law, when the next in line appeared to be Lord Curzon, the Foreign Secretary. The king thought that in the twentieth century the Prime Minister should sit in the Commons, not the Lords, and accordingly Curzon,

[1] The Prime Minister is referred to as 'he' throughout for the sake of convenience, though the election of Mrs Margaret Thatcher as leader of the Conservative Party in February 1975 shows that the possibility of a woman Prime Minister cannot be ruled out.

to his bitter disappointment, was passed over. Again in 1940 George VI chose Winston Churchill to succeed Neville Chamberlain, when his personal preference was for Lord Halifax, because he felt in wartime the Prime Minister must sit in the Commons. The choice has not always been between a member of the House of Lords and a member of the House of Commons. In 1957 Harold Macmillan became Prime Minister on the retirement of Sir Anthony Eden, when many people thought that R. A. Butler was the stronger candidate. Nor has the Commons always won against the Lords, for in 1963 Lord Home was chosen to succeed Macmillan (the favourite was again Mr Butler) when he was still a member of the House of Lords (Lord Home subsequently disclaimed his peerage, see p. 54).

It now seems clear that should a Prime Minister resign or die while in office, the party to which he belonged would insist on electing a new party leader. The man or woman chosen would then be asked by the monarch to take up the office of Prime Minister. If the Queen exercised her prerogative of choice in defiance of the party's wishes, it is almost certain that the party involved would refuse to accept her candidate. In the same way if, after an election, the monarch asked a politician who was not the party leader to become Prime Minister, he would probably be unable to form a government, and one cannot be a Prime Minister without an administration.

Another interesting point concerning the monarch's powers is the question of the dissolution of Parliament. Parliament is dissolved by the monarch but can only be dissolved with its own consent. Opinions differ as to whether the monarch is bound to give the Prime Minister a dissolution just because he asks for one. It is thought to be legitimate for a Prime Minister to ask for a dissolution if he feels that he does not have a large enough majority to allow the Government to carry on its business, as Harold Wilson did in 1966, when his majority was three, and again in 1974 when he was the head of a minority Government. However, if a Prime Minister asked for a dissolution for a frivolous reason, or when the Opposition was split to such an extent that it could not provide an alternative Government, it is possible that the monarch would refuse to grant the request. But in the latter case, if the Prime Minister refused to continue and no other member of his party agreed to form an administration, and if the Opposition was completely incapable of forming a Government, the result would probably be chaos and a dissolution. The whole process would undoubtedly do much to discredit Parliament and the cry would go up that the Crown was being involved in politics.

Politics in this context means of course party politics, with the implication that the Crown would be called upon to express a preference for one party rather than another. In the past, of course, monarchs were often blatant in their support for one party (or one politician) rather than another, but in modern times the monarch has been expected to be completely neutral as far as parties and personalities are concerned. (It is generally acknowledged that Queen Victoria detested the Liberal leader W. E. Gladstone and distrusted his party, but nevertheless she was compelled to accept him as her Prime Minister on no less than four occasions.) At the present time a Labour Government is as acceptable to the Crown as a Conservative Government (or indeed any other government). As we have seen the Government is Her Majesty's Government and the ministers are Her Majesty's Ministers, taking their office from the Crown. The relationship of the Opposition to the Crown is also acknowledged by the fact that it is termed Her Majesty's Opposition. Thus although the Government and the Opposition may oppose each other's philosophies and policies they both owe loyalty to the Crown which represents the British constitutional system. The point is further underlined if one considers the membership of the Privy Council, the body entrusted with the duty of proffering advice to the monarch (see also p. 21). The leaders and many of the senior members of both the government and opposition parties are Privy Councillors, along with other distinguished personages of varied political affiliation (or none at all).

This lack of political involvement can have some curious side effects. Each session of Parliament opens with the Queen's Speech, which contains details of the Government's programme for the session. Thus if a Labour Government was in power the Speech might propose legislation for nationalisation and increased state intervention in the planning of the economy. The next year a change of political fortune at the polls might mean that the Queen's Speech contained a Conservative programme to denationalise industry and reduce state intervention.

The monarch must also be careful about becoming involved in politics when no party has an absolute majority, so that a coalition must be formed. In practice this situation seldom arises in British politics, for reasons that will be explained later.

While the Queen undoubtedly has private views she must ensure that they remain private; on virtually every controversial issue the Queen and other members of the royal family have to maintain a discreet silence. If the Queen makes a public statement she does so on the advice of her ministers, and the statement will have been prepared by them. Just as ministers are expected to advise the monarch on controversial matters, so the monarch has the right to advise ministers and it is probably here that the monarchy retains the last of its political power. The monarch is, except in the rare event of abdication, on the throne for life, whereas ministers have a much shorter tenure of office. Over the years a monarch can build up a great deal of experience in government, because each day state papers and other important documents are delivered to the palace, for perusal by the Queen in her capacity as Head of State. She also holds regular audiences for the Prime Minister and other ministers, who are expected to tell her what is happening in their departments and in the Government as a whole. Queen Victoria, who came to the throne in 1837 and died in 1901, accumulated a considerable amount of expertise about the constitutional process, and was only too willing to proffer advice to her ministers.

A question that has received considerable attention in recent years is whether the monarchy is too expensive. In 1952 when Queen Elizabeth II ascended the throne Parliament debated the question of the Civil List and agreed to grant the Queen an annual sum of £475,000. The greater part of the Civil List was earmarked for household expenses and salaries of members of the household, though £95,000 was a supplementary provision to take care of inflation. In January 1972 the Civil List was revised and under the new arrangements the Queen received £980,000. Three years later it was considered that inflation had eaten into this to such an extent that the Civil List was raised to £1,400,000. The Civil List is free from income tax, though the Queen pays tax on income from her private estates.

The Queen is granted the Civil List in return for handing over the Crown Estates to the Exchequer, and this has happened since the time of George III. Although the Crown Estates officially belong to the Crown no monarch could keep them if for some reason he considered that the Civil List was inadequate. By convention the monarch hands over the Estates, and convention in this context has virtual force of law. Nor do the Crown Estates belong to the monarch as personal property, for most of them date from the time, still preserved in the usage 'Royal' and 'Her Majesty's', when the state and Crown were almost indistinguishable.

Nevertheless the Queen has a considerable personal fortune, in addition to jewels, paintings and a stamp collection that is said to be worth over a million pounds. She owns two of the royal residences, Balmoral and Sandringham (when Edward VIII abdicated in 1936 his brother, who became George VI, had to buy them from him), though Buckingham Palace and other royal palaces, such as Windsor Castle and Holyrood House in Scotland, are maintained by the state. The state also pays for the Queen's aircraft, maintained by the Royal Air Force, the Royal Yacht, which is part of the Royal Navy, and various administrative expenses.

In return for the royal salary, for that is what the Civil List amounts to, the Queen is expected to fulfil her constitutional duties and also to undertake tours and visits in Britain, the Commonwealth and foreign countries. It is in this area that the Queen and her family have a very important role to play, for the British royal family enjoys considerable prestige, both at home and overseas. People seem to be attracted by the aura of monarchy and the glamour that accompanies it. There is little doubt that the royal family is a great tourist attraction, and Buckingham Palace is an object of pilgrimage for many visitors to Britain, particularly for those staunch republicans, the Americans.

The glamour of monarchy is also seen in its connections with the House of Lords and the orders and decorations that are granted in the royal name. Britain is one of the few countries where the aristocracy retains a certain amount of political power, and the Crown's role in the maintenance of this power is of considerable importance. In earlier times the monarch enjoyed the right to give titles to anyone he liked, and a number of the present members of the House of Lords owe their seats to the fact that one of their ancestors was a sovereign's favourite. Today peers are created on the advice of the Prime Minister, who will also consult the leaders of the other main political parties. The Queen is also responsible for all other honours that are given in her name, such as knighthoods and the membership of various orders, though once again these are given largely on political advice. There are, however, one or two orders that are reserved for those who have given special services to the sovereign.

It can be argued that the monarchy, because of its close connection with the aristocracy and its aloofness from everyday life, contributes to social divisions within society, but few Englishmen seem to be in favour of its abolition. If a newspaper article or book is published that is even mildly critical of the royal family, there is an outcry, and all kinds of terrible punishments, from incarceration in the Tower of London downwards, are suggested for the unfortunate author. But such a fate seems unlikely at the present time; indeed it was interesting to see that one of the most outspoken critics of the monarchy, the MP William Hamilton, was interviewed on both television and radio when his controversial book *My Queen and I* was published in 1975.

THE PRIVY COUNCIL

It is the Privy Council's duty to offer advice to the monarch, and it is through the Council that he or she exercises statutory powers. In addition to having this advisory function the Privy Council also discharges certain other duties not directly concerned with the monarch.

Today its functions are almost completely ceremonial, though it is considered a great honour to be invited to become a Privy Councillor. All Cabinet Ministers receive the title on assuming office for the first time, and distinguished public figures from Britain and the Commonwealth are invited to become Councillors on the recommendation of the Prime Minister. Membership of the Council is for life, and there are usually about 300 Councillors at any one time, all of whom are entitled to be called 'The Right Honourable . . .', and put the letters PC after their names.

The Council is presided over by the monarch (or in the absence of the monarch, by Counsellors of State). Officially a quorum is three, though in practice meetings are rarely attended by fewer than four Councillors. The Council only meets as a whole on important occasions such as when the sovereign dies.

The Privy Council has a number of committees, and it is out of these in the past that departments of state have grown, for example the Department of Education and Science. The most important committee of the Privy Council today is the Judicial Committee and there are also committees concerned with the Channel Islands, the Isle of Man, the universities of Oxford and Cambridge, the Scottish universities, the granting of charters to municipal corporations, and the baronetage.

PARLIAMENT

The British Parliament consists of a lower chamber, the House of Commons, and an upper chamber, the House of Lords. It sits in the Palace of Westminster – probably better known as the Houses of Parliament – which is situated between Westminster Abbey and the River Thames.

Parliament has the following responsibilities: it passes legislation, it provides the finance necessary for the running of the state, and it brings forward important issues for discussion by the Commons, or the Lords, or both. It also ratifies international treaties and agreements to which Britain becomes a party, though in theory the making of treaties is the prerogative of the sovereign. Parliament is, in short, responsible for governing the country, and this government is carried on by agreement between the political parties elected to the House of Commons by the citizens of the United Kingdom. The majority party forms the Government and the minority party the Opposition. Thus the minority party accepts the right of the majority party to run the country, while the majority party accepts the right of the minority party to criticise the way this is being done. Without this tacit agreement between the political parties the British parliamentary system would break down. It is also important to realise that the Opposition is an alternative Government and its members are potential ministers.

Members of the House of Commons are chosen by the people, at elections, but members of the House of Lords sit by right, as peers of the realm. To be passed by Parliament a Bill must go through both Houses, and then it must be approved by the

THE SYSTEM OF GOVERNMENT IN BRITAIN 23

monarch before it can become law. The details of this process will be discussed later.

The two Houses of Parliament are responsible for arranging their own affairs, free from interference from the Crown, or any other outside body, and these privileges, won over the centuries with great difficulty, are jealously guarded. Ultimately who sits in the Commons is decided by the electorate and each Member of Parliament is responsible to the voters of his own constituency. However, Members of Parliament are not delegates, but representatives, that is they do not have to put into force a policy that has been decided by the people who have chosen them. As representatives they can act as they think fit, only being accountable for their stewardship at elections. There have always been those who feel that MPs should be more closely answerable to the views and opinions of the electorate and on occasion steps have been taken to bring pressure on the Members concerned. In practice this has meant that the local constituency party claiming to represent the electorate of the constituency has challenged the MP and his views, for example in the case of Mr Reg Prentice, a right-wing member of the Labour Cabinet who was disowned by his local Labour Party in mid-1975. Another case of potential outside pressure is when MPs are sponsored by trade unions. The unions expect the Members to follow the union line if they want to keep their sponsorship. Until the referendum of June 1975 there was no provision under the British system of government for any form of direct democracy. The decision to hold a referendum caused disquiet among some MPs because they felt that it would undermine the powers of Parliament. In the event the voters supported Parliament's decision on EEC membership and so no conflict arose. It is, however, interesting to note that since June 1975 suggestions have been put forward for referenda on other issues. As yet none of these have been taken up. Voters of course have the right of direct access to their MP and can bring matters of importance to his notice. In this way the individual Member of Parliament is the vital link between the citizens and government.

The Political Parties
The British electorate choose their representatives in Parliament at 'general elections' or 'by-elections'. At the former all parlia-

mentary seats are contested, and there must be a general election at least every five years. A by-election occurs when a seat in Parliament falls vacant, owing to the death or 'resignation' of Member and an election is held to select a new Member for that particular seat. In theory electors vote for an individual, and until recently the ballot paper on which people recorded their vote made no mention of political parties. In fact most people seem to vote for the candidates of one or other of the political parties, and the overwhelming majority of the electorate tend to see the choice as lying between two parties, Labour and Conservative.

It is often claimed that the British Parliament depends on the 'two-party system', with one party forming the Government and the other the Opposition. This is something of an oversimplification, as can be seen by looking at the results of the October 1974 election, when Members of Parliament representing seven different parties were returned. However it is true to say that the Labour and Conservatives won far more seats than any of the other parties. Labour had 319 seats and the Conservatives 277, while the next largest party was the Liberals who won 13 seats. An interesting feature of this election was the return of 14 nationalist MPs, 11 for the Scottish Nationalist Party and 3 for Plaid Cymru (the Welsh Nationalist Party). The 12 Northern Ireland seats at Westminster were won by 10 Ulster Unionists, an Independent and a member of the (Northern Ireland) Social Democratic and Labour Party. The reason why the Conservative and Labour parties have such a large number of seats compared with the other parties can be found in the voting system, which we will examine shortly.

The Conservative and Liberal parties can trace their origins back to the Tories and Whigs of the seventeenth century, but it is only comparatively recently that the modern parties, with their elaborate bureaucracies for paid organisers and agents, have developed. Until the last years of the nineteenth century the Conservatives and Liberals were the only parties elected on a national basis to the House of Commons (there were a number of Irish Nationalists sitting for Irish seats, but they were primarily concerned with Irish affairs). In 1867, 1884 and 1885, working-class men were given the vote and in the 1890s a number of socialists were returned. By the first decade of the twentieth century the Labour Party had become a significant force in British politics. During the inter-war period the Labour Party displaced the Liberals as the second party in Parliament, though quite a sizeable Liberal 'rump' persisted up until the Second World War.

In 1945, following the end of hostilities in Europe, an election was held which was won by the Labour Party, by 393 seats to the Conservatives' 213. The Liberal Party was reduced to a mere 12 seats. The 1950 election resulted in another Labour victory, though with a much reduced majority, and the following year the Conservatives were returned to power. The Conservatives won the 1956 and 1959 elections, but they were turned out in 1964 by the Labour Party which won with a majority of three seats over all other parties. In 1966 a further election was held which gave the Labour Party a majority of 96. Four years later it was the turn of the Conservatives, who won by 30 seats, and they held office until February 1974, when the Labour Party became the largest single party in the House of Commons, with 301 seats. If the Conservatives (296 seats) had been able to do a deal with the Liberals (14 seats), they could have formed a coalition which would have given them a majority over the Labour Party. But the Liberals were unwilling to ally themselves with the Conservatives and the Labour leader, Harold Wilson, formed a Government. Running the country with a minority Government proved to be extremely difficult, and in October a new election was held. In this election the Labour Party gained a majority of three seats over all other parties.

The Conservative Party can loosely be described as the party of the middle and upper classes, the party of the property-owner and the businessman. Much of the money used for financing party campaigns, at both local and national level, comes from large industrial concerns, and many Conservative MPs sit on the boards of leading companies. However a number of studies have shown that a substantial number of the working class consistently vote Conservative. The reasons for this are not entirely clear, but it has been suggested that in some cases people have improved their social position to some extent, and voting Conservative is one way of demonstrating this. Others, it is thought, vote Conservative because they feel that Conservatives are 'gentlemen' and as such have a better understanding of the way government works. This attitude seems to be found mainly in country areas. The Conservatives draw most of their support from rural areas, small towns and the residential suburbs of large cities.

The Labour Party has always had strong links with the trade union movement and much of its financial backing comes from this source. Some unions nominate candidates for particular seats, making themselves responsible for election and other expenses. This support is of considerable importance to the party, as for obvious reasons they cannot rely on assistance from large industrial combines.

The Labour Party draws most of its support from the working class, but also attracts votes from certain sections of the middle class and a core of intellectuals (many of whom are members of the Fabian Society), who are regarded with considerable distrust by some party members. The traditional Labour voter, however, is the industrial worker, who is also a trade unionist. The Labour Party is strongest in industrial areas and the towns.

As we have seen, it is the Labour and Conservative parties which dominate British political life at the present time. Due to a voting system which discriminates against small parties, anyone who wishes to become an MP finds that the only way he, or she, is likely to realise this ambition is to be adopted by one of the major political parties. One result of this is that the party labels, Labour and Conservative, cover groups within which there are often very diverse opinions. Both the Conservative and Labour parties can be regarded as coalitions, in which members of the party broadly agree with the party line and accept the discipline of the party structure. It is probably true to say that the left wing of the Conservative Party is nearer the right wing of the Labour Party than the right wing of its own party, and under a different electoral system it is conceivable that they would both break away from their parent parties and combine with the Liberals to form a 'Centre Party'. In the same way it is possible that other groups within the parties on both left and right would reconsider their political loyalties, should the majority vote system ever be discontinued.

As we have seen at one time the second large party in Parliament was the Liberal Party. During the twentieth century, however, it has been replaced by the Labour Party, for while the

Conservatives seem to have been able to adapt to changing circumstances, the Liberals appear unable to find a role in modern conditions. After an impressive start in the Liberal administration of 1906 to 1916, the party virtually tore itself apart during and after the First World War. Even so, the Liberal Party has not disappeared completely, and according to some optimists the Liberal revival is merely a matter of time. A number of spectacular by-election results have served to reinforce these hopes, while in February 1974 the Liberals won 6,056,713 votes, 19·3 per cent of the popular vote. By October, however, this was down to 5,348,193 votes, 18·3 per cent. There is little doubt that the voting system is biased against the Liberals for even with a large vote, as in February 1974 they won only 14 seats.

Of considerable interest in recent years has been the rise of the nationalist parties in both Scotland and Wales. Although Plaid Cymru (the Welsh Nationalists) and the Scottish Nationalist Party regularly put up candidates for Parliament during the fifties and sixties, they rarely attracted many votes. However in recent years support has been growing and in the second election of 1974 the Scottish Nationalists won 11 seats, while their Welsh counterparts won 3. Both parties want independence from England – though opinions differ among members as to how complete this independence should be – and the right to set up their own Parliaments. In the case of the Scots a great deal of force has been given to their claims for economic independence by the discovery of oil in the North Sea, oil which the nationalists consider is Scottish rather than British, and which has currently overtaken whisky as Scotland's most important liquid asset.

The dominant party in Northern Ireland is that of the Ulster Unionists and ten of the province's MPs belong to the party. At one time the Unionists were closely affiliated to the Conservative Party, but the troubles that have afflicted Northern Ireland since 1969 have led to a breach between the Conservatives and Unionists.

The Communist Party has no seats in Parliament at the present time, though during the inter-war years, and again in 1945, Communist MPs were returned. There are a number of extreme right-wing parties, which if they trouble to stand at elections usually take a strong anti-immigrant line.

The House of Commons

Elections The members of the House of Commons (Members of
Parliament) are elected by those of their fellow citizens who
have attained the age of eighteen, and who are not specifically
disqualified from voting by law (see p. 29). General elections
must take place at least every five years, though there is no
fixed date on which an election must be held. In practice the
choice of the election date almost invariably rests with the
Prime Minister of the day, and it is obvious that he will choose
a time that will give his party the maximum advantage. As we
have seen, a Prime Minister with a valid reason for a dissolution
(and valid reasons are not difficult to find) would encounter no
difficulty from the monarch, so within the limits of the five-year
rule a Prime Minister has considerable scope for manoeuvre.
One factor that may restrict his freedom of action is the size of
his majority, for the inability to carry through a legislative
programme can bring down a Government more quickly than
anything else. Given a reasonable majority, however, a Government can put itself in a strong position when a general election
is due. Apart from the great advantage of selecting the date, the
Government can arrange its legislation in such a way that the
period immediately before an election sees measures that will
make the administration popular with the voters. There is of
course the danger that if the Government is too generous the
opposition parties will immediately suspect that the thoughts
of the Prime Minister are turning towards the ballot box.
Indeed, by the time a Government enters its fourth year,
parliamentarians, political commentators and the general public
are all keeping a close eye on events in the hope of finding out
when the next election will occur.

Once the Prime Minister has decided that the time has come
for an election he asks the monarch for a dissolution and Parliament is then terminated by Royal Proclamation. Polling day is
seventeen working days from the date of dissolution. As soon
as Parliament has been dissolved the Lord Chancellor issues
writs for the holding of fresh elections throughout the country,
and these writs are sent to the returning officers in each parliamentary constituency. In urban constituencies the returning
officer is the chairman of the district council, in rural constituencies the sheriff of the county performs the duties of the office.

In Scotland the appropriate officer is the sheriff and in Northern Ireland, the under-sheriff. The returning officer appoints a deputy returning officer, usually the clerk of the council, and it is this official who actually arranges the election. Details of arrangements for the election must be published by the returning officer by 4 p.m. the day after the writs have been issued.

The election is now formally under way and all those concerned in it have been informed of the fact. The most important participants are of course the voters, who are actually responsible for choosing the MP. Each constituency has a register of voters and this is brought up to date in November each year. This enables new electors to be entered on the register, while people who are no longer resident in the constituency have their names removed, for the vote depends on residence, i.e. everybody votes in the constituency in which he lives. Until 1948 some people had two votes; if they lived in one constituency and had business premises elsewhere they were entitled to a business vote, while graduates of the older universities could vote for 'university seats'. These forms of voting were abolished by the Representation of the People Act of 1948, and so it is only from this date that Britain has fully accepted the principle of 'one man, one vote'. Even today there are a few exceptions to this principle. Apart from those under eighteen years of age, peers and peeresses in their own right, persons of 'unsound mind' and felons (those serving criminal sentences of more than twelve months) are not allowed to vote. Also excluded are people who have been involved in electoral offences. People who are away from home for a valid reason on polling day, or who are serving overseas with the armed forces, can make arrangements to vote by post or proxy.

A consituency usually consists of about 60,000 voters, though as the population may change from one election to the next there is a Boundary Commission, which constantly reviews constituency boundaries and recommends adjustments when necessary. Thus constituencies may disappear or alter in size, while entirely new seats may be created, and these changes may also produce a change in voting patterns. In 1974 there were 516 constituencies in England, 36 in Wales, 71 in Scotland and 12 in Northern Ireland.

If the electors are the most important actors in the election drama, next in order of importance are the candidates. Any man or woman over twenty-one can be a candidate at a parliamentary election, with the following exceptions: peers and peeresses in their own right, lunatics, felons and those who have committed electoral offences, i.e. the same categories as those excluded from voting, with the following additions: clergymen of the Church of England or the Roman Catholic Church, undischarged bankrupts and those holding 'offices of profit under the Crown'. The last includes civil servants and members of the armed forces; if they wish to stand for Parliament they must first resign from their posts.

Once he has decided to stand, the prospective candidate must fill in nomination papers, which contain his full name and occupation, and these are then signed by a proposer, a seconder and eight other electors for the constituency in which the candidate is standing. The nomination form must be handed in to the returning officer not later than the eighth day after the proclamation summoning the new Parliament. The candidate must also produce a deposit of £150, which he will lose unless he receives at least one-eighth of the votes cast in that constituency. The purpose of this deposit is to discourage frivolous candidatures.

Once the candidate has declared himself he has to convince the voters that he is the best man to be their MP, and indeed if he is wise he will have been doing so for some time before the election. As has already been pointed out, virtually all the seats at a general election are fought on a party basis. The candidates are selected by the local party organisation, and are then supported by this organisation in their fight for the seat. Both of the major parties have a branch in nearly every constituency and the Liberal Party also has a large number of local organisations. If the candidate wins the seat the local party continues its support, often providing him with an office where he can interview constituents, and secretarial assistance. In both main parties the local parties are responsible for the selection of candidates, though the central organisation can intervene if it considers that the choice is totally unsuitable or damaging to the party's prospects. The local parties, however, guard their independence jealously, and central interference is relatively rare. In most cases the local constituency party supplies the candidate with an agent, and it is his responsibility to direct the election campaign in that particular constituency. Some wealthy constituency organisations have salaried full-time agents. Those that are less well off rely on a part-time agent, or someone recruited for the period of the election. The agent arranges meetings at which the candidate can meet the public and get his policies and personality over. The agent is also responsible for arranging 'canvassing', the backbone of election work, which consists of the candidate and his helpers knocking on doors and asking the voters for their support. There is a certain amount of disagreement over how effective canvassing is, but there are few agents who would have the courage to suggest that it is unnecessary. Another important duty of the agent is to keep an eye on expenditure, to ensure that election expenses do not exceed the legal limit, which is £1,075+£0·05 per six electors in county constituencies and £1,075+£0·06 per eight electors in borough constituencies. The candidate must declare any personal expenses above £100.

The local party is greatly helped if its candidate has been the MP for the constituency in the previous Parliament. Even if he has not been particularly effective, his name will probably be better known than those of his opponents, who might well have visited the constituency for the first time on the evening of their adoption meeting. (Candidates do not have to live in the constituency they stand for, though many buy or rent a house there if they are elected.)

Studies have shown that at national elections people tend to vote for a party rather than a man, and therefore it is important that the candidate is identified with the party for which he is standing. It has been estimated that when all the candidates are standing for the first time in a constituency, their individual characteristics only make a difference of a few hundred votes. Of course a few hundred votes can be of great importance in the simple majority vote system, as is illustrated by the following example from Caithness and Sutherland (Scotland) in the 1945 election:

E. L. Gander Dower (C)		5,564
R. McInnes	(Lab)	5,558
A. Sinclair	(Lib)	5,503
		———
Conservative majority		6

The Conservative was elected, even though the Labour candidate received almost as many votes as he did. If the Labour and Liberal votes are added together it will be seen that nearly twice as many people voted against the Conservative as voted for him. It is an interesting feature of the British system that it is not uncommon for an MP to represent a constituency in which more people have voted against him than have voted for him, though the results are not always as dramatic as in the example given above.

Another disadvantage of the majority vote is that it does not accurately reflect the wishes of the electorate as a whole, as a party can win a larger share of the popular vote than its opponents, but still end up with fewer seats. This is due to the fact that in many constituencies a large number of votes are 'wasted': a candidate returned with a majority of one is just as much a Member of Parliament as a candidate who gets a majority of 20,000. Another feature of the present system is that a small party may get a large number of votes at a general election in the country as a whole but the voters will be spread out over more than 600 constituencies and therefore the number of seats actually won will be out of proportion to the support they can muster. These points are illustrated by the election results for 1951 and February 1974.

In 1951, although the Labour Party received more votes than the Conservatives, the Conservatives won more seats:

	Votes	Seats	% of votes
Conservative	13,717,538	321	48·0
Labour	13,948,605	295	48·8
Liberal	730,556	6	2·5
Others	198,969	—	0·7

Thus the Conservatives formed the Government.

In February 1974, however, the result was:

	Votes	Seats	% of votes
Labour	11,661,488	301	37·2
Conservative	11,928,677	296	38·1
Liberal	6,056,713	14	19·3
Others	1,695,315	23	5·4

In this case the Labour Party won fewer votes than the Conservatives, but five more seats. There were also thirty-six MPs

who belonged to neither the Conservative Party nor the Labour
Party. (The thirty-seventh 'other' was the Speaker.) For a few
days it was far from clear what was going to happen. While the
commentators discussed the pros and cons of minority governments and coalitions, the politicians vied with one another to
give their interpretation of the electorate's wishes. It was only
after the Liberals rejected the idea of entering a coalition with
the Conservatives that Edward Heath, the Conservative Prime
Minister who had called the election, decided to resign, giving
up the seals of office to Harold Wilson.

The position of the Liberals in the February 1974 election
was extremely interesting. Although they received 19·3 per cent
of the vote, compared with 2·5 per cent in 1951, they only increased their representation in the Commons by eight seats, as
their supporters were scattered throughout the United Kingdom.
The 'others' however won twenty-three seats with 1,695,315
votes. The reason for this is that twenty of these were nationalist candidates, Scottish Nationalists, Plaid Cymru and Ulster
Unionists, standing in their home areas. There was therefore
very little wastage.

It is because of results like these that some people have asked
for a review of the electoral system. Some advocate the introduction of proportional representation, arguing that PR is more
democratic as it reflects more accurately the wishes of the voters.
Not unnaturally the supporters of PR are usually found among
the members of the smaller parties, particularly the Liberals.
However it is debatable whether in the long run the PR system
is more democratic. It is true that with this system more parties
are represented in Parliament, but rarely is one party large
enough to form a Government on its own. A coalition of two
or more parties must therefore be set up and a coalition usually
means a compromise on policy, so that members of a coalition
may have difficulty in fulfilling their election programme. A
voter who voted for a socialist party, for example, might see
his party and its programme swallowed up by a 'Centre' party
coalition. It is generally thought that it was the unwillingness of
the Liberal Party to compromise their position that kept them
out of the coalition offered by the Conservatives in February
1974. Although there were probably those among the Liberal
MPs who relished the idae of achieving ministerial office, there
was little doubt that the bulk of the party's rank and file mem-

bership were opposed to an alliance with the Conservatives, or indeed any other party.

It is, of course, true that if a member of a coalition objects to the coalition's policy it can withdraw from the partnership, but this points to another weakness of the PR system, the danger of unstable governments. In Britain a Government usually manages to remain in office for a number of years, during which it succeeds in getting a legislative programme through. It could be argued that too large a majority means that the Government will pass its legislation without sufficient regard for the opinions of the country, but it should also be remembered that the Government is accountable to the electorate at frequent intervals. If a Government does not heed the wishes of the voters when it is in power, those voters may well turn it out of office when election time comes round.

Another interesting feature of British elections is that relatively few voters change their opinions from one election to the next, and indeed most seem to vote consistently for one party all their adult life. It could therefore be argued that the propaganda issued by the parties is mainly directed at the minority who may change their minds, at the 'floating voters'. Election propaganda takes many forms. Virtually all the parties issue an election manifesto which lays down their aims and policies and these are discussed and quoted at great length during the campaign at public meetings, on radio and television and in the press. Each candidate also prepares an election address, which is distributed to each voter in his constituency, and consists of a localised version of the party's manifesto, together with questions of particular interest to that constituency.

The whole national campaign comes to a head on polling day, which is customarily a Thursday. Polling booths are open from 7 a.m. until 10 p.m.; but polling day is not a holiday, so workers have to vote on the way to work, or in the evening. After all the votes are cast they are counted by tellers, and the result is then announced by the returning officer. Interest is usually concentrated on 'marginal seats', for just as relatively few voters change their party allegiance there are certain seats that are more likely to change hands than others. A seat like Deane Valley, Labour majority 27,269 in October 1974, is almost certain to remain Labour, while there seems little chance that Worthing (Conservative majority 17,345 in 1974) will ever return an MP of a party other than Conservative. Each party has a number of these 'safe' seats; it is the 'marginals' that can go either way, and these decide the result of the election.

Formation of the Government   Once the election is over the monarch calls upon the leader of the victorious party to form a Government. Having accepted the invitation, the new Prime Minister goes to his official residence, 10 Downing Street (given by George I to Sir Robert Walpole, the first Prime Minister) and begins the intricate business of choosing the ministers who will help him in his task of administering the country. First of all the Prime Minister will choose the most important ministers, those who go to make up the Cabinet. There are no hard and fast rules as to how many ministers there are in the Cabinet. In fact, the size of the Cabinet has been growing throughout the century, in spite of repeated declarations by Prime Ministers that they intend to reduce its size in the interests of efficiency.

One problem that faces the Prime Minister when he selects his colleagues is deciding what areas of government are important enough to warrant representation in the Cabinet. Some ministers such as the Chancellor of the Exchequer, the Foreign Secretary and the Secretary of State for Education and Science must obviously be given Cabinet seats, but the decision is more difficult when it comes to the Secretary of State for Scotland, for example. There are those who would say that he could well be left out, but with seventy-one seats in Scotland, many of which are vulnerable to Scottish Nationalists, it is a brave Prime Minister who would exclude him. Then there are the debts that have to be paid to the different sections of the party, the left wing and the right wing, or smaller internal groups. As has been explained, both the large British political parties are to a certain extent coalitions. This means that the Prime Minister must select his colleagues from all sections of the party, for if a powerful group is ignored there will inevitably be dissatisfaction. The Prime Minister must always remember that he is also the party leader, and ultimately his position depends on his party's support. So for several days the cars of potential ministers block Downing Street, while the Prime Minister examines the hand the voters have dealt him, and from which he must form his Government. At the end of the period of interviewing and consulting, the Prime Minister will have his Cabinet consisting of some twenty ministers, and a further seventy to eighty junior ministers.

When they have been appointed, ministers go to Buckingham Palace, to be received by the monarch and kiss hands on appointment. The Cabinet Ministers will also be sworn in as Privy Councillors, if they are not members of the Council (see p. 21) already. Most of the important ministers will be members of the Commons, but the Prime Minister must remember that he has obligations to the Lords as well, and some ministers will come from the Upper House, the most important of them being the Lord Chancellor.

If the party that was in power before the election is returned to power the construction of the Government is far easier. However the Prime Minister may use the election as an excuse to effect some changes, while it is always possible that the voters may have forced changes upon him.

Although both the Conservative and Labour Parties have 'Shadow Cabinets' (the Conservatives prefer the term 'The Leader's Committee') when in opposition, consisting of the leading Opposition spokesmen on important issues, membership of this in no way guarantees them a place in the Government if the party comes to power.

The Cabinet   The Cabinet consists of the leading ministers of the Crown, though its membership is decided by each Prime Minister individually. The Cabinet usually has around twenty members, though sometimes there may well be a smaller unofficial group comprising an 'inner cabinet'.

Cabinet meetings are usually held every Wednesday morning in the Cabinet Room at 10 Downing Street, though in an emergency they can be held anywhere. Discussions at these meetings are secret, and although minutes have been kept since the First World War, they are not published for thirty years. In certain cases retired senior ministers writing their memoirs have been allowed access to the Cabinet records in order to refresh their memories, and this has sometimes resulted in details of Cabinet meetings being made known before the period of thirty years has elapsed. However ex-ministers are expected to observe certain conventions. The late Richard Crossman, who served as a Labour Cabinet minister, gave detailed accounts of Cabinet meetings and also his relations with civil servants in his diaries.

Although extracts from the diaries appeared in a Sunday newspaper during 1975 the question of the publication of the complete book was referred to the courts. In September 1975 permission was granted by the High Court for publication to go ahead and the first volume came out at the end of the year.

The Cabinet is the body responsible for discussing and deciding Government policy, and as such is the heart of the government system. It is presided over by the Prime Minister and it is he who is responsible for directing the course of meetings. Discussion is free, and very often, so we are led to believe, heated, but eventually the Cabinet works out a policy that is acceptable to all. No vote is taken, but agreement is reached or assumed to be reached. Once a certain course of action has been approved by the Cabinet it becomes Government policy, and all ministers accept responsibility for it, even though they may have been in bitter opposition in the Cabinet meeting. This concept of Cabinet unanimity and collective responsibility is very important, and if any minister feels that he cannot accept a particular decision he has no alternative but to resign. In early 1975 the Labour Prime Minister, Harold Wilson, announced that during the run-up to the referendum on the EEC ministers would be permitted to express their personal opinions on the question of membership, a decision which caused much criticism.

Functions and Procedure of the House of Commons At first sight a Member of Parliament's job does not seem to be particularly arduous, and it appears that he earns his salary of £5,750 a year for very little actual work. Members also receive a secretarial allowance of £3,200. On weekdays from Monday to Thursday the House of Commons does not meet until 2.30 p.m., and it usually adjourns at 10.30 p.m., though if necessary the House can, and does, sit through the night. On Fridays the House assembles at 10 a.m., and sits until 4.30 p.m., rising early so that MPs can visit their constituencies at the weekend.

Attendance in the Chamber, however, is only one part of parliamentary work. In addition an MP must sit on parliamentary committees, deal with the problems of his constituents, keep himself informed about affairs at home and overseas, and travel both in Britain and abroad, so a conscientious Member will find that he has very little spare time.

Many MPs combine their work in Parliament with another job; for example, many barrister MPs still practise in the courts, while others, particularly on the Conservative side of the House, are engaged in business. There is considerable support for this practice, usually on the grounds that it helps Members to keep in touch with the outside world, but there are many who feel that perhaps some Members devote too much time to interests outside Parliament, and that their parliamentary work suffers.

Once a Member of Parliament has been elected he cannot resign his seat until the next general election. However if for some reason he is unable to continue as a member he can apply for the post of Bailiff or Steward of the Chiltern Hundreds or the Manor of Northstead. These positions are technically offices of profit under the Crown, though they carry no actual duties, and acceptance of such office disqualifies the holder from membership of the House. Having left his parliamentary seat the ex-Member then immediately resigns the Stewardship. In some cases of course this procedure is unnecessary because a Member has been appointed to a genuine office of profit.

One of the first things a newly elected MP will find is that his 'seat' does not really exist. The Chamber of the House of Commons is too small to accommodate all the Members, and when an important debate is taking place MPs may have to find places on the stairs or in the gangways. During the Second World War the Houses of Parliament were damaged by enemy action and there were those who believed that the opportunity should be taken to rebuild the Chamber of the Commons on a more generous scale. However Winston Churchill, who was responsible for the rebuilding, insisted that it should be restored as before, on the grounds that if the Chamber was enlarged the atmosphere of the Commons would be lost, and debates would be more difficult to follow.

The Chamber is designed with the two-party system in mind. The Government sits on one side of the House, with the Opposition on the other side, facing it. The leading ministers sit on the front bench of the Government side of the Chamber, while directly opposite them are ranged the leading spokesmen for the Opposition. Behind the 'front benchers' sits the rank-and-file MPs, the 'back benchers'.

Between the two rows of benches sits the Speaker, the chairman of the House. He is selected from among the Members of

Parliament, and on being chosen renounces his party allegiance, to become the servant of the whole House. Because of his non-party position it is customary for the Speaker to be re-elected to subsequent Parliaments without having to contest his seat. However on a number of occasions candidates have stood against the Speaker on the grounds that the Speaker's constituents have been disenfranchised, as their MP cannot take part in parliamentary debates. Recently it has been suggested that once the Speaker has been selected by his fellow MPs he should then resign his seat and be transferred to a titular consistuency with no electors, but so far no move has been made to implement this suggestion. At one time the Speaker was appointed by the Crown and controlled debates on his royal master's behalf. Even today the Speaker is expected to show reluctance to assume office, and at the installation ceremony two Members are deputed to drag him to his chair. While acceptance of the office inevitably means the end of a political career, it has considerable compensations in terms of prestige for a Member who is prepared to accept the fact that he will never achieve Cabinet rank. On ceremonial occasions the Speaker represents the House of Commons and the importance of that institution is recognised by the fact that he takes precedence over all except the royal members of the House of Lords.

The Speaker is no longer a royal nominee and the Crown has lost most of its power to Parliament, but it is nevertheless still the sovereign who opens each session of Parliament with the Speech from the Throne. Each autumn the Queen drives to the Houses of Parliament and ascends the throne in the House of Lords – though technically the throne is not *in* the House of Lords. The Commons are summoned from their Chamber by the Gentleman Usher of the Black Rod. On receiving the summons the members of the House of Commons file through the Palace of Westminster, headed by the Prime Minister and the Leader of the Opposition, to take their place at the bar of the House of Lords. The contents of the Queen's Speech will hold no surprises for the Prime Minister, as he and his colleagues will have been responsible for compiling it. For the other people in the Chamber, and in the country outside, the speech will be of considerable interest for it contains an outline of the legislation the Government intends to introduce during the session. After listening to the speech, the Commons return to their own

Chamber for a debate on its contents, during which the Opposition will give its reactions to the Government's proposals.

The State Opening of Parliament obviously owes much to tradition, and there are many who say that the whole procedure is out of date today; some MPs have even suggested that when Black Rod comes to call them to go to the Lords they should refuse. However the problem is that so much of the recognised procedure for conducting the business of Parliament is based on precedent and custom that to revise part of it would entail revision of the rest, and this might well upset the delicate balance between the different sections of the legislative machine. In addition to custom and precedent both Houses of Parliament have their own standing orders, and it is the duty of the Speaker to bear all these elements in mind when conducting the business of the Commons. The Speaker, or his deputy, is responsible for supervising debates and the voting that takes place when the debate is over. He announces the result, and in the rare event of a tie he has the casting vote.

From Bill to Act   There are four main classes of parliamentary Bills: Public Bills (Finance Bills), Public Bills (Non-Finance Bills), Private Members' Bills and Private Bills.

Public Bills are those which affect the whole community and can, in theory, be introduced by either the Government or the Opposition. In practice since most Public Bills involve the spending of money they are nearly always introduced by the Government. Private Members' Bills are introduced by individual MPs, while Private Bills deal with the interests of a local authority (i.e. in local government), a company or an individual.

Public Bills   Before a Bill is introduced to the House, its main outline and the principles it embodies are discussed by the Cabinet and other ministers involved. Once agreement has been reached on the basic form of the Bill, it is drafted by a team of ministerial experts and lawyers. When the Bill has been prepared the minister who is responsible for it gives notice of its intended introduction and on the appointed day the formal First Reading takes place. There is no discussion at this stage; the minister merely accepts responsibility for the Bill and the Clerk of the House reads out the title. A day is given for the Second Reading and the Bill is sent to the printers. Afterwards it is circulated to all Members so that they can study it in detail.

When the day for the Second Reading arrives the minister in charge makes a speech explaining the aims of the Bill and why it had been introduced. At the end of his speech he proposes that 'the Bill be read a second time', and it is at this stage that the debate on the Bill begins in earnest. If the Bill is an important one it is customary for the first reply to come from the leading Opposition spokesman on the matter in question, and his speech will present his party's views on the issue. The minister and the Opposition front bencher speak from a position near the dispatch boxes, which are kept on the table of the Clerk of the House, but back benchers speak from where they are sitting. By convention only front benchers use notes; other Members are expected to rise from their seats and give extempore speeches. The rules of parliamentary debate are strict and are closely adhered to. Members are addressed by the Speaker and their fellow Members by the names of their constituency; thus Sir Harold Wilson is referred to in debate as 'The Right Honourable Member for Huyton' (if Sir Harold were not a member of the Privy Council he would be merely 'The Honourable Member for Huyton'). If a Member is referred to by name during a debate it is a rebuke from the Speaker, for a 'named' Member has offended against the rules of the House, and is liable to suspension. Barristers, in addition to being 'Honourable' are 'Learned', while retired members of the armed forces are 'Honourable and Gallant'. Parliamentary procedure also distinguishes between words and phrases that are permitted and those that are not. For example Winston Churchill once called a fellow Member a liar; on being told that 'liar' was an unparliamentary word, Churchill withdrew it and said that the Member had committed 'a terminological inexactitude', which amounts to the same thing.

The debate continues until all those who have some contribution to make have spoken, or until it is felt that proceedings must be drawn to a close because time is running out. Lack of time is one of Parliament's greatest problems, and so usually only a Bill that proposes radical changes in the law will be given sufficient time for all those interested to speak. Even so, Members are expected to keep their contributions brief, and an MP who continues for more than ten minutes will find that his audience is getting restless. Debates are usually brought to an end by the House rising at 10 p.m., but if necessary the House can sit after this time, even right through the night. If a Member proposes that 'the question be now put' and the proposal is accepted by at least a hundred Members the debate is brought to a close.

Sometimes it is felt necessary to speed the passage of a controversial Bill through Parliament by the use of the 'guillotine' or the 'kangaroo'. In the case of the former a timetable is worked out for the Bill and this is strictly adhered to, even though all those who want to speak on the issues it embodies have not been able to do so. The kangaroo is a procedure whereby the Speaker, or Chairman of Committees, select only the amendments which he thinks represent important sections of opinion, so that the debate does not get bogged down over relatively unimportant matters. These methods are not used too frequently because if they were, Members might suspect that the Government was trying to limit debate on controversial topics. The Speaker can also intervene to cut short a long-winded speech or one that is irrelevant, which means that the opportunities for 'filibustering' are limited.

When the debate is ended the question is put by the Speaker. Those in favour call out 'Aye', those against 'No'. The Speaker judges the relative strength of these verbal responses and announces the result. Frequently however there is disagreement with the Speaker's interpretation and a Division follows. Division bells ring all over the Palace of Westminster (and in at least one public house nearby, not to mention some flats and houses in Westminster owned by MPs) and every MP who hears the bell is expected to drop what he is doing and rush to the Chamber to vote. Six minutes after the bells have been rung the doors of the Chamber are locked and the Members file out through the division lobbies, the 'Ayes' to the right, and the 'Noes' to the left. As the Members pass through the lobbies they are counted by tellers, who then report the numbers to the Speaker so that he can announce the result of the voting.

In theory each MP has the right to decide into which lobby he will go, but on most occasions he is expected to 'follow the party line'. If he is a member of the party that is in office he is expected to vote for Government legislation, while if he is an Opposition member he is expected to vote according to the directives of the party, which usually means against the Government. If a Member votes in defiance of the instructions issued by the party he is likely to find himself in serious trouble with the Whips. Each party has a Chief Whip who, with the Assistant Whips, is responsible for maintaining party discipline. (The name is derived from the 'whipper-in' in fox-hunting, whose job it is to ensure that the hounds are kept under control.) The Government Chief Whip is also the holder of a ministerial post, Parliamentary Secretary to the Treasury. The Chief Whip and his assistants act as middle-men between party opinion and ministers, and play an important role in ensuring that communications are kept open between the front bench and their supporters. If controversial legislation is planned it is the duty of the Whips to make sure that the party will support the leadership and to give ample notice of any potential rebellion. The Government Chief Whip is not a member of the Cabinet but he attends Cabinet meetings, so that Cabinet Ministers can be given up-to-date information about party attitudes and morale. The Whips' Office is also responsible for ensuring that there are enough MPs from the party available if a Division is called. The Opposition Whips will always try to have sufficient MPs to defeat the Government, while the Whips on the Government side have to ensure that there are always enough of their Members present to prevent this happening. Whips also ensure that there is a quorum in the Chamber. If there are fewer than forty Members present a Member may challenge the quorum, the Division bells are rung, and if sufficient Members do not appear within four minutes the House is adjourned.

If a Member cannot attend a debate which is expected to end in a Division he must make arrangements to ensure that his absence will not affect the vote. He does this by finding a member of the opposing party who will also be absent and arranging a 'pair', so that they cancel each other out. On certain occasions, such as when a very important debate is taking place, the pairing system is suspended, as all parties expect their MPs to be in the Chamber, or at least within range of the division bells. Each week every MP belonging to a major party receives a letter from the office of his party's Whips. The letter (also known as a whip) contains details of parliamentary business for the next week and informs the Member how important it is for him to be at Westminster. If a major debate is in the offing all parties will insist that Members cancel engagements outside London, or at least ensure that they can get back in time for the Division. So that there is no confusion over what items are considered to be of prime importance they are underlined three times, hence the expression a 'three-line whip'. A two-line whip is customary if the business is not so pressing, and in this case a Member's presence is requested unless he is paired. A one-line whip indicates that it is thought unlikely that a vote will take place.

To defy a three-line whip is tantamount to defying the party leadership. Such action will almost certainly lead to an inquiry, which could in turn lead to expulsion from the party, unless a really convincing explanation is given. It might be considered that the power exercised by the Whips is a gross interference with the freedom of the individual MPs, but the party system depends upon party unity, and should this break down organised government would soon prove impossible.

In virtually every Parliament there are MPs who leave or are expelled from their party. Sometimes the break is final. There are even cases where Members have crossed the floor of the House to join the opposition party, though on other occasions the Whip is rejected or withheld only temporarily. If a former party member has not returned to the fold by the next general election it is probable that the local constituency party will have adopted a new candidate to fight the seat. The retiring MP then has a choice of withdrawing or standing as an independent. While, as we have seen, it is difficult for an Independent to conduct a campaign against the organisation of the major parties, it is interesting to note that in a number of cases an MP who has been rejected by his local party has nevertheless succeeded in carrying the electorate with him and has been returned as an Independent.

For example, early in 1973 Mr Richard Taverne, who had resigned from the Labour Party and subsequently left Parliament on the Common Market issue, was re-elected by the voters of Lincoln with a handsome majority. Taverne hoped that this was the beginning of a new force and possibly a new 'Social Democratic and Labour' party in British politics, but in 1974 he was defeated in a general election.

Should the Government be defeated on a Bill or if its majority is low, there will inevitably be cries of 'resign' from the Opposition, who will claim that the Government has lost the confidence of the public. However a Prime Minister is not bound to resign if his Government is defeated on a single occasion, particularly if the defeat is the result of a snap Division, or because bad weather conditions have prevented Government MPs from reaching the House. However any defeat is a grave psychological blow and the Whips' Office is expected to ensure that the full voting strength of the party is available when it is required. The task of the Whips is particularly difficult when the Government's majority is small or nonexistent, as was the case between February and October 1974.

In practice, a Government with a comfortable majority can be virtually certain of getting its Bills passed, particularly if they are dealing with important issues. If the Government sees that a measure is arousing too much opposition it may decide to withdraw it until a more favourable opportunity presents itself.

After the Second Reading the Bill moves to the Committee Stage, where it is taken apart and discussed in detail, clause by clause. Important Bills, including all Finance Bills, are considered by a Committee of the Whole House. When this occurs the mace, the symbol of the Speaker's authority, is placed below the Clerk's table, and the Speaker vacates the chair, to be replaced by a chairman who conducts the ensuing discussion in a more informal manner than when the House is debating a motion. The Committee ends when the motion 'That the Chairman do report progress and ask leave to sit again' has been passed. The mace is then restored to its usual position and the Speaker resumes his chair. Less important Bills are dealt with by the five or six Standing Committees. These committees consist of between twenty and fifty MPs selected from all parties, in the ratio in which their parties are represented in the Commons. Committees usually sit in the morning, in special rooms in the Palace of Westminster, and tend to be very time-consuming. The Committee reports back to the House after it has considered the Bill, and it is at this stage that the amendments proposed by the Committee are either accepted or rejected by the proposer, while further amendments can also be put forward. Not infrequently a Bill is referred back to the Committee for further discussion. (Standing Committees must not be confused with Select Committees, which are appointed to inquire into and report to the House on special matters. Select Committees may be appointed for a particular purpose, or they may be appointed at the beginning of a session in order that they are in being to consider any issues that might arise during the session. Sessional committees include the Select Committee on Estimates and the Committee of Privileges.)

After the Committee Stage the Bill is given a Third Reading, and if it is passed it goes to the House of Lords. Here it goes through the same stages as it did in the Commons, though if the Lords propose amendments that alter the nature of the Bill, it must be returned to the Commons for further discussion. The Lords may not reject a Finance Bill, nor can they delay any other Bill for more than one session. The implications of this are discussed in the section on the House of Lords. If a Bill has been initiated in the House of Lords it must then go to the House of Commons for discussion.

Once a Bill has been passed by the Lords it is given the Royal Assent. This assent is usually given in Letters Patent and then announced by the Speakers of both Houses. Once this has been done the Bill becomes an Act. Although in theory the sovereign can refuse to give consent to a Bill, in practice this right has not been exercised since the early eighteenth century, during the reign of Queen Anne.

Private Bills   Private Bills are usually promoted by local authorities, though personal Private Bills can be put forward by any citizen or group of citizens. However, largely due to the expense of briefing a lawyer to defend the Bill in Committee and the cost of getting a Bill drawn up in the first place, personal Private Bills are rare today. Private Bills introduced by local authorities usually deal with land purchase, and often concern the taking over of graveyards or obtaining the necessary powers for development.

Private Members' Bills are Bills introduced by individual Members of Parliament. At the beginning of each session a ballot is held, and MPs who come high enough in this are permitted to introduce a Bill on a matter that is of particular interest to them. A number of Fridays are set aside for the discussion of Private Members' Bills, but only those who come reasonably high in the ballot will stand much chance of getting their Bill debated. Some of these Fridays are reserved for the

First Reading of Private Members' Bills and the remainder for later stages, so even if a Member gets his Bill through the First Reading it may get no further.

Apart from time there are other factors that work against Private Members' Bills. In the first place the Bill must be drawn up, a difficult task requiring expert advice, because a badly worded Bill will be torn to pieces by critics. Even when he has his Bill, and parliamentary time to introduce it, the troubles of the would-be legislator are not over. One of the rocks on which many Private Members' Bills founder is the 'counting out' of the House, for there are no party Whips to ensure that there is a quorum. This is a common way for opponents of a Bill to stop its progress, for attendances on Fridays are often very poor. Another problem may be that instead of there being too few MPs interested in the Bill, there are too many. As we have seen there are relatively few days available for the discussion of Private Members' Bills, and if the opponents of a controversial Bill can make the debate stretch out, the end of the session may be reached before the Bill has been passed. A Bill that has not completed its passage through Parliament in one session must be reintroduced and the whole process begun all over again. The only way to get over this difficulty is for the Government to give parliamentary time to enable a Bill to be discussed. Private Members' Bills dealing with controversial matters that the Government of the day is, for one reason or another, unwilling to introduce, but to which it is broadly speaking sympathetic, may therefore be debated and passed outside the time reserved for Private Members' Bills.

If a Member is unlucky in the ballot for Private Members' Bills he still has an opportunity to introduce a Bill under the 'ten-minute rule'. Any Tuesday or Wednesday, at the end of Question Time, an MP may propose his Bill and speak in favour of it for ten minutes. After he has spoken any other Member can speak against his Bill for the same amount of time. The Speaker then 'puts the question', and if the House accepts it this First Reading is considered complete. The problem now faced by the proposer is to find the time for the next stages of the Bill. If it can be classified as 'unfinished business' it can be dealt with during the Debate on the Adjournment, provided that no other Member objects, for the opposition of a single MP is enough to stop it on this occasion. The main purpose of the adjournment debate is to allow Members to raise important business. At 10 p.m. the House completes the business it has been discussing, and the motion 'That this House do now adjourn' is proposed, which leads to a further debate on some question of Government policy, or any other matter not requiring legislation. Other motions to adjourn may be on matters of great public importance, which cannot be debated at any other time. A member of the Government can put forward such a motion immediately after Question Time, before any other item on the Order Paper (i.e. the order of business for the day) is taken. Any other Member may also propose an emergency motion at the same time, but if this motion is to be accepted it must be supported by at least forty other Members. If he succeeds in getting the support required the motion is debated at 7 p.m., and takes precedence over all other business. An emergency debate can, if necessary, continue after the normal time for the adjournment of the House at 10 p.m.; however such debates only take place if the Speaker is convinced that a case for urgency has been made.

Question Time, mentioned in the last section, gives the individual MP another opportunity to have an influence on the conduct of the Government. Question Time takes place at about 2.40 p.m. every day immediately after Private Business, and lasts for about an hour. Two days' notice of questions must be given, and most questions are answered in writing. If he wishes, however, a Member can insist that the minister to whom he is putting his question answers it orally in the House of Commons. When the question has been answered the Speaker allows supplementary questions, and often a skilled questioner will reserve the full force of his question for the supplementary, thus hoping to catch the minister off-guard. If the Member is still unsatisfied after pursuing the matter about which he is concerned in a supplementary, he can give notice that he will raise it again on the adjournment.

Parliamentary Questions are of considerable importance in the British system of government, because they give individual Members a chance to keep a check on the executive. All ministers, from the Prime Minister downwards, are liable to be questioned, and on some occasions an apparently harmless question has revealed a highly unsatisfactory state of affairs. More than once a minister has had to resign as a result of information that was first brought to light by a Parliamentary

Question. Not all questions are of such a dramatic nature, however, and many are the result of a constituent complaining of an injustice to his MP, who then follows the matter up with a question to the minister concerned.

All the business of the House as outlined above takes place in public, except on rare occasions when matters of national security are discussed. A record is kept of all debates and questions and these are printed in the Official Report, known to all as Hansard, after the printer who was appointed to do the job in 1812. At various times it has been suggested that proceedings in the House should be televised, but each time the proposal has been defeated. However in 1975 it was agreed that there should be some radio transmissions for a trial period and the first of these took place in June of that year.

The House of Lords

The upper chamber of Parliament is known as the House of Lords and its membership is made up of the Lords Temporal, hereditary peers and life peers; and the Lords Spiritual, the bishops of the Church of England.

The largest group are the hereditary peers, that is men (and a few women who are peeresses in their own right) who possess hereditary titles. They fall into several different categories. In the first place there are the royal Dukes, members of the royal family who have seats in the Lords, but who in fact rarely participate in debates. Next come the non-royal Dukes, the senior of whom is the Duke of Norfolk, hereditary Earl Marshal of England, whose title dates from 1483. Dukes are followed by Marquesses, who are comparatively rare, and then come Earls, Viscounts and Barons. All these titles pass to the next male in line on the death of the holder; if there is no heir the title dies out. Although the aristocracy has existed since Norman times few of the present titles are very ancient, virtually all of them being post-1600. At one time kings found titles a convenient way to reward favourites, while at some periods of history titles have been sold openly, or with very little attempt at concealment. The early Stuarts, for example, used the sale of titles to bolster their revenues when Parliament was reluctant to grant them money.

At the present time there are just over 1,000 people who have the right to sit in the House of Lords (about 200 of these are life peers, 26 are bishops and archbishops of the Church of England and the rest are hereditary peers), though not all of them choose to do so. In addition to the royal Dukes a number of other peers apply for, and are granted, leave of absence. There are probably fewer than 200 peers who take a regular part in debates, though others will attend if they are particularly interested in the subject that is under discussion. The creation of peers is the prerogative of the sovereign, but in practice it is the Prime Minister who decides whether new peers are to be created, and who they should be.

Life peerages were introduced in 1958. As the name suggests life peers hold their titles for the duration of their lives and the title becomes redundant on death. Although it is the Prime Minister who draws up the lists of new peers it should not be thought that he recommends only members of his own party to the monarch. When new peers are created, for example in the Dissolution (of Parliament) Honours or in the New Year Honours, the other party leaders are asked to make their recommendations. Nevertheless party politics plays an important part in the Lords and one of the problems faced by a Labour administration is that there is a massive Conservative majority in the Upper House.

Churchmen have sat in the Lords since its earliest days, and at one time the abbots from the leading monasteries attended as well as the bishops. Today the Lords Spiritual consist of twenty-six Anglican bishops: the Archbishops of Canterbury and York, the Bishops of London, Winchester and Durham, and twenty-one other bishops in order of seniority. The bishops sit as representatives of the Established Church, the Church of England. There is no provision for other churchmen to sit in the Lords, though a prominent Methodist minister was made a life peer some years ago. It has been suggested that a similar honour should be bestowed on the Roman Catholic Archbishop of Westminster, but as yet the proposal has not been put into effect.

The ten law lords, who comprise the supreme judiciary of Great Britain, sit in the House by virtue of being Lords of Appeal in Ordinary. They are life peers and when they retire as law lords they retain their seats. Their functions are dealt with in Chapter 4.

Unlike MPs, members of the House of Lords are not paid a

salary, though they can claim an allowance of up to £13.50 for each day they attend debates. The House of Lords sits shorter hours than does the Commons, and does not sit on Fridays.

The House of Lords is presided over by the Lord Chancellor, who sits on the Woolsack (a large cushion stuffed with wool from Britain and the Commonwealth; wool was Britain's most important export in the Middle Ages). He fulfils the same functions as the Speaker in the House of Commons. However unlike the Speaker the Lord Chancellor is an active politician, appointed by the Prime Minister and with a seat in the Cabinet. He is also head of the legal profession and has important functions associated with this position, as we shall see when we look at the legal system. When the Lord Chancellor wishes to participate in a debate he leaves the Woolsack, and his place is taken by another member of the House, usually the Chairman of Committees.

Functions of the House of Lords The House of Lords has two main functions: it is the second chamber of Parliament with the right to discuss legislation; and it is also the highest court in the land.

Until the beginning of the twentieth century the House of Lords was theoretically equal in status to the House of Commons, though in fact it was clear that all major decisions were made by the Lower House. The last Prime Minister to sit in the Lords was Lord Salisbury, who resigned in 1902.

In 1911 the Parliament Act was passed which placed limitations on the power of the Lords. The Act said that the Lords could not in future reject a Bill that had been passed by the Commons, though they could delay it for two years. Money Bills had to be passed within a month of their coming from the Commons. (The Act also contained some clauses not directly related to the issue of the Lords, including providing a salary for MPs and making a reduction in the life of Parliament from seven to five years.)

However the 1911 Act did not seem to have the desired effect, as the Lords still obstructed Bills, and even today when the delaying power of the Lords is only a year (since 1947) some Bills are halted by the Upper House simply because the Commons does not have the time to discuss them again. (A Bill rejected by the Lords must go all the way through the Commons again, even though it has already been passed there once.) Of course the Government will find time for a Bill that it considers important, but some measures are in effect killed by the Lords. Private Members' Bills in particular often run into difficulty in the Upper House. As the Lords still has a large Conservative majority a Labour Government can suffer considerable obstruction from the Lords, as was seen when the Wilson administration was in power from 1964 to 1970. Few peers would want to risk a head-on collision with the Commons, but they have a number of ways in which they can delay Government business if they wish, ways that are more subtle than outright rejection. In 1967 proposals were made to reduce the power of the Lords, and in 1969 a proposition was debated that would have restricted the voting rights of hereditary peers. However when it became obvious that to get the proposed Bill through would entail a major parliamentary battle, lasting many months, the plans were dropped.

So the House of Lords survives, and there are many who would support its existence. It is often claimed that the Lords provides a useful second opinion on legislation; amendments can be suggested and new opinions expressed. Another argument in favour of the Lords is that as they have more time than the Commons they can discuss a Bill in far greater detail. It is also frequently suggested that this discussion can be freer than it is in the Commons, because the Lords do not have constituencies to worry about, or electors to offend, and so they can speak more freely on controversial issues. This is a rather peculiar argument, for it draws attention to the fact that the Lords represent nobody but themselves. It also raises the whole question of whether Parliament should take public opinion into account, and whether Parliament is, or should be, responsible to the people – a question of vital importance to a democracy (see also p. 14).

The introduction of life peers in 1958 produced another argument in favour of the retention of the House of Lords. It was suggested that the Lords might become a forum of experts, and that distinguished men who did not have the time or inclination to fight an election or nurse a constituency could still be recruited to give the country the benefit of their experience. This is an interesting argument in theory, but it is not borne out in practice. Although it is true that some eminent doctors, scientists and academics have become life peers, most have been chosen from the ranks, or at least the fringes, of the political parties. Nor does this argument explain why hereditary peers should retain the right to sit in the House of Lords.

As far as the Prime Minister is concerned the House of Lords certainly has its uses. He can use it as a dumping ground for Members of Parliament who have safe seats but little political value. The ennoblement of such a man vacates the seat, which then can be allocated to a potential minister. The Lords can also be used by the Prime Minister to bring new blood into the Government when a by-election might prove embarrassing. The Prime Minister can make the man he wants a life peer, thus providing him with a seat in the House of Lords.

An argument frequently put forward in favour of the retention of the House of Lords is that the Lords safeguards the constitution. According to this argument it is claimed that the Commons could, if they were so inclined, change the whole British system of government in an afternoon by a single majority vote. This argument means of course that the Lords, who as we have seen represent only themselves, exist to protect the British people against their elected representatives. Should the Lords be abolished it might be thought necessary to introduce safeguards into the system to limit the power of the Commons, but these could probably be arranged without much difficulty. In some countries for instance constitutional changes require the approval of the people in the form of a referendum, while in others such legislation can only be passed if the representative chamber approves the measures by a large enough majority, usually in the order of two-thirds. There seems no reason why similar procedures could not be adopted in the United Kingdom, particularly as the referendum device has already been used in relation to Common Market membership.

Until recently peers who inherited titles were forced to accept them whether they wanted to or not. Thus politicians who were making a name for themselves in the House of Commons might suddenly find that they were elevated to the House of Lords, where they would get prestige and the guarantee of a seat in one of the legislative chambers, but would stand little chance of gaining the highest political office. A number of men who found themselves in this situation had complained bitterly about it, but had resigned themselves to what they considered to be the inevitable. However in the early sixties Mr Anthony Wedgwood Benn, a prominent Labour MP, found himself transformed overnight into Viscount Stansgate when his father died. In spite of his objections he was told that he had no option but to give up his parliamentary seat in Bristol and take his place in the House of Lords. He accordingly vacated his seat, but at the ensuing by-election he stood as a candidate and was returned with a comfortable majority. He then tried to take his seat in the Commons, but was refused admittance to the Chamber. An electoral court subsequently awarded the seat to the Conservative who had been runner-up. Wedgwood Benn's campaign, however, had aroused considerable interest and sympathy, and in 1963 the Peerage Act was passed. Under the terms of this Act a person who inherits a peerage is permitted to disclaim it for his lifetime, and on his death it passes to the next in line. The first person to take advantage of the Act was of course Lord Stansgate who speedily returned to the Commons, and in due course became a Cabinet Minister.

Shortly after the Act was passed a prominent Conservative, Viscount Hailsham, renounced his title in the hope of becoming leader of the Conservative Party and Prime Minister on the resignation of Mr Macmillan. As Quintin Hogg he was elected MP for Marylebone, but in the event the leadership went to another member of the Lords, the Earl of Home, who became Prime Minister as Sir Alec Douglas-Home. Subsequently both these gentlemen have returned to the Lords as life peers, as Lord Hailsham of St Marylebone and Lord Home of the Hirsel.

MINISTRIES

In recent years a number of 'super-ministries' have been established, some of which incorporate smaller ministries which at one time had a separate existence. For example the Department of the Environment includes ministries responsible for transport, local government and housing. Each of the 'super-ministries' is headed by a Secretary of State, and he is assisted by a number of junior ministers, ministers of state and under-secretaries of state.

Each ministry is staffed by civil servants under a permanent secretary. The civil servants are responsible for advising their ministers and for putting the decisions taken by the politicians in Parliament into effect. In theory civil servants do not take decisions themselves, but in practice they wield considerable power. Much of their power comes from the fact that while the minister holds his job for a relatively short period of time, the civil servant is a permanent official who over the years can acquire considerable expertise in his field. Many have expressed considerable misgivings about the growth in the influence of Whitehall (the area of London where most of the important ministries are found), and one of the tasks of the Fulton Committee which reported in 1968 was to see whether far-reaching reforms were required. A number of Fulton's recommendations have been put into effect, though whether these will produce any significant changes as far as the role of civil servants is concerned is not yet clear.

The reader will find reference to a number of Royal Commissions in this book. Royal Commissions are committees set up by the Government to investigate and make recommendations on various matters. They invite evidence from interested individuals and bodies; this is sifted and then examined and a report is issued. The Government is not bound to accept the advice of a Royal Commission.

3

Local Government

During the last few years a great deal of attention has been paid to the question of local government reform. No less than three Royal Commissions, appointed to inquire into the problems of local government in different areas of the country, presented their reports during the sixties: the Royal Commission on Local Government in London in 1960; the Royal Commission on Local Government in England, and the Royal Commission on Local Government in Scotland in 1969. A fourth Royal Commission that might well have an effect on the structure of local government reported in October 1973. This was the Kilbrandon Commission on the Constitution, which among other things recommended the setting up of assemblies with limited powers for Scotland and Wales. It also suggested that some form of regional self-government should be established within England, though in view of the recent local government reorganisation it seems unlikely that this section of its proposals will be put into effect. Talks have taken place to discover the most appropriate form of assembly for Scotland and Wales, but it is apparent that the wishes of the nationalist groups (and other groups within both countries) are somewhat at variance with those of Westminster which is only in favour of limited devolution.

The reason for this flurry of activity was that it was becoming increasingly evident that a system of government established in the nineteenth century, in many cases on the basis of institutions that had existed for hundreds of years, was no longer appropriate for dealing with the complex functions of local administration required in the modern world.

The traditional units of English local government were the parish, the borough and the county. As is the case with so many other British institutions, they originally fulfilled functions far different from those that they were later called upon to undertake. The parish was in its early days an ecclesiastical unit, the centre of which was the parish church. During the sixteenth and seventeenth centuries it acquired civil functions, such as the maintenance of highways and care of the poor. Borough status was granted by the Crown. Apart from the prestige of receiving a charter, the honour was a coveted one because it gave towns a certain amount of independence. Boroughs had their own courts, and they could also hold markets and send representatives to Parliament. The county was originally the territory granted to an earl by the king in return for feudal service. In spite of the fact that a feudal lord's fief is not necessarily the most suitable basis for modern administrative purposes, the basic outline of the English counties, particularly in the south of the country, has varied little from the Middle Ages.

In 1835 boroughs became the first local government units to acquire some degree of democracy. The Municipal Corporations Act provided for a system of local councillors elected by ratepayers, while a quarter of the council were 'aldermen', elected by the councillors. The Local Government Act of 1888 introduced a system of county councils, elected by ratepayer franchise as in the boroughs. The Act also clarified the relationship between local and national government and between county and borough councils. Although the idea of an elected county council was new, the areas of the counties remained much the same as they had been prior to 1888, the only major change being that some of the larger counties were subdivided. Thus shortly after the Act was passed sixty-two county councils had been formed from the fifty-two geographical counties.

The structure of local government established in the nineteenth century remained in force until well into the twentieth. In 1966, however, a Royal Commission on Local Government was appointed and its report was published in 1969. In essence it proposed a sweeping away of the old local authorities, replacing them with a system of fifty-eight unitary and three metropolitan authorities. The Maud report, as it was called after its chairman Lord Radcliffe-Maud, was much discussed at national and local level. In 1970 the Labour Government produced a White Paper in which it accepted the proposals of the Commission, though with a number of modifications. But before the Government could make these reforms law Labour was defeated at the General Election of July 1970. The incoming Conservatives produced their revised plans for the reform of local government in February 1971, and in 1972 the Local Government Reorganisation Act established a new pattern of local authorities which came into effect on 1 April 1974. There are six metropolitan counties: Greater Manchester, Merseyside, West Midlands, West Yorkshire, South Yorkshire and Tyne-Wear; 39 non-metropolitan counties; and Greater London. Both the metropolitan and the non-metropolitan counties are subdivided into districts, of which 36 are in metropolitan counties and 296 in non-metropolitan councils. County councils are responsible for planning, roads, public transport, waste disposal, consumer protection and police and fire services. County councils outside metropolitan areas and district authorities inside metropolitan areas are responsible for education, youth employment, personal social services and libraries. Housing, local planning, building regulations, collection of waste and a number of other powers are under the control of district authorities. Museums and art galleries, conservation areas, airports and the acquisition and disposal of land for planning purposes are subject to control by both district and county authorities.

In many cases the boundaries of the old administrative counties have remained the same, though some smaller ones have disappeared, while some larger units have been divided up, particularly in the north of England. In general an attempt has been made to fix the minimum population of the new counties around the quarter of a million mark. Metropolitan counties outside London range in population from just over 1,200,000 for Tyne-Wear to nearly 2,800,000 for the West Midlands.

In 1958 a Commission for Wales was appointed to review local government in the principality, and this Commission proposed that the number of Welsh counties should be reduced from thirteen to seven. The proposal aroused strong opposition and was shelved, but in 1967 a new report recommended that counties should be merged and several county boroughs should be reduced in status. Following the publication of the Maud report still further changes were put forward and since April 1974 local government in Wales has been in the hands of eight counties.

The local government reorganisation caused considerable heart-searching among many local authorities and their representatives, as boroughs and councils that had histories stretching back many centuries found that their identity was being swallowed up in a new authority with an unfamiliar name. Some people found they regretted the widespread introduction of politics into local government, often conveniently ignoring the fact that councillors who had sat for years as 'Independents' were in fact members of, or sympathetic to, political parties.

Local councils consist of a number of elected councillors presided over by a chairman. Some districts have the ancient rank of borough, now purely a ceremonial title, and some are known as cities. In boroughs the chairman is granted the courtesy title of Mayor while in certain large or ancient cities he is the Lord Mayor (in Scottish burghs the titles are Provost and Lord Provost). Councillors hold office for four years; in counties they stand for electoral divisions, in districts for wards.

Expenditure by local authorities is financed from the following sources: grants from central government, local rates and rents from council houses and flats, dividends and interest. The size of the government grant depends on the size of the council and the number of people it must provide for. Another factor that is taken into account is the age composition of the population, particularly the numbers of old and young people, as education and old peoples' homes are provided by local authorities.

Rates are a form of tax levied on occupants of non-agricultural land and buildings. The amount each ratepayer contributes is calculated by multiplying the rateable value of his property (i.e. roughly the amount the property would bring in if it was to be rented out) by the rate poundage (a percentage fixed by the authority according to its anticipated needs). Rates are paid by the head of the household, and although other people living in the house may contribute to the sum required there is no obligation for them to do so. This means that if a man lives by himself in a house his rate bill may well be the same as that of his next-door neighbour who is married and has three grown-up children living with him. (Even so, lodgers who do not pay rates are still entitled to vote in local elections.) Recently the rates system has come under a considerable amount of attack, particularly as a new assessment introduced in April 1973 led to huge increases in rate demands. It seems that before long a new system will be brought in, though as yet there is not general agreement on the form it should take.

Loans are used to finance capital expenditure and are raised by issuing mortgages or selling stocks and bonds on the Stock Exchange. Local government borrowing powers are closely supervised by central government.

4

The Legal System

The legal system of England and Wales has evolved over a considerable period of time. Its origins can be traced back to before the Norman Conquest of 1066. Whereas in many countries there is a criminal and civil code, in England and Wales the two main elements of law are common law, which is largely dependent on precedent, and statute law, which consists of Acts of Parliament (though the division between criminal and civil law is fully recognised). Scottish law differs from that of England and Wales in a number of important respects, and the procedure and officials of the Scottish courts are peculiar to that country.

COURTS IN ENGLAND AND WALES

Criminal Courts

Since the Courts Act of 1971 came into force at the beginning of 1972, there have been two levels of criminal courts in England and Wales. Magistrates' courts deal with the great majority of criminal cases, while more serious offences are dealt with by the Crown courts, which replaced the Assizes and Quarter Sessions.

Magistrates' Courts Magistrates' courts are (except in London and a few large towns) presided over by lay Justices of the Peace, who sit on the bench part-time, and receive no salary for their services. The jurisdiction of the magistrates' courts is local, counties being divided into petty sessional divisions, while each town of any size has its own court. The court has three main functions. First, it hears and determines charges against people accused of summary offences, that is offences that are not serious enough to go before higher courts. The magistrates' courts may also try certain indictable offences, offences of a more serious nature, with the agreement of the accused. Normally indictable offences are tried by a court with a jury, but in some cases the accused person may prefer to have the case dealt with by the two to seven magistrates sitting on the bench in the lower court. This may be to the advantage of the accused if he is found guilty, as the sentences imposed by a magistrates' court are less than those of the higher court. On the other hand there is a chance that a jury will take a more sympathetic view of the offence than the magistrates, and decline to convict. About 98 per cent of all criminal cases are disposed of in the magistrates' courts.

The second function of the magistrates' court is to conduct a preliminary hearing, to decide whether there is sufficient evidence to commit the accused for trial in a higher court. Thirdly the magistrates hear cases involving children. Juvenile courts hear cases in which children under 14 are brought before the court as being in need of care and protection. They also administer justice in criminal proceedings brought against young people between the ages of 14 and 17.

In addition to these judicial functions the magistrates act as licensing authorities for public houses, restaurants, betting shops and other public places.

There are about 19,000 lay magistrates, sitting in nearly 1,000 different centres. As the magistrates rarely have any formal legal education there are frequently considerable discrepancies between sentencing policy in different parts of the country. Some studies have shown that while the magistrates in one court will be particularly hard on one offence, magistrates in another place will adopt a far more liberal attitude. Factors such as this have led many people to criticise the system, and to suggest that magistrates' courts should be replaced by courts presided over by professional lawyers. However the lay Justice of the Peace has a history dating back to the fourteenth century, and there are many, including most magistrates, who would be loath to see the office disappear.

In spite of the fact that magistrates are unpaid and only receive small allowances, there is no shortage of people who would like to sit on the bench. Appointments are made by the Lord Chancellor on the recommendation of a local committee for each area, and in theory anyone without a criminal record can become a JP. In practice most magistrates tend to be middle-class people, and the great majority of them are over fifty years old. One is far more likely to find a retired doctor or army officer presiding over a magistrates' court than a plumber or engine-driver, retired or still at work. Nor has the old role of the Justice of the Peace as the country gentleman been entirely forgotten and many magistrates, particularly in country areas, are appointed on what appears to be an almost hereditary basis. A large number of JPs are people who are, or have been, prominent in local government or 'public life', and appointment to the bench is often regarded as a recognition of public service, as it confers considerable social prestige.

Since 1966 it has been compulsory for newly appointed justices to participate in training courses, and to attend court as observers before actually taking their seats on the bench. Even so the magistrate still relies a great deal on the guidance of the magistrates' clerk, who is a lawyer appointed as legal adviser to the bench, and in all except the smallest courts a full-time official.

Stipendiary magistrates In London and a few of the larger provincial cities there are full-time stipendiary magistrates (as well as JPs) who sit alone. The stipendiary magistrates – there are thirty-seven in London and a further eleven in other cities – are trained lawyers and unlike their lay counterparts they receive a salary. Suggestions have been made that the use of stipendiary magistrates should be extended, but the proposal has been resisted by the legal profession, who claim that there are not enough lawyers, and the lay magistrates who are reluctant to see their powers reduced.

Crown Courts In 1966 the Government established a Royal Commission to prepare a report on Assizes and Quarter Sessions, under Lord Beeching. In 1969 the report was published and as a result the Courts Act was passed in 1971. By this Act the ancient courts of Assize and Quarter Sessions, which had their origins in the thirteenth century, were abolished, and in their place Crown courts were set up.

Under the old system Quarter Sessions were held in each of the counties of England and Wales, in ninety-three boroughs and Greater London, and the City of London. In the counties cases were heard before magistrates who sat under a legally qualified chairman. In the boroughs with their own Quarter

Sessions the proceedings were presided over by a Recorder, who was responsible for passing sentence, though guilt or innocence was decided by a jury of twelve. Juries were also found in the courts of Assize, which were branches of the High Court, presided over by a High Court judge. The courts of Assize were held in assize towns (usually the county town of each county) and in other large towns or cities. For the purpose of the assize the country was divided into seven 'circuits'. The judge allocated to the circuit visited each assize town in turn, each town was visited at least once, the larger ones twice. The Assize court for Greater London was the Central Criminal Court, sitting at the Old Bailey, which was in continuous session.

The new system of Crown courts retains the circuits, but these have been reduced from seven to six. The new circuits and their administrative centres are: south-eastern (London), midland and Oxford (Birmingham), north-eastern (Leeds), Wales and Chester (Cardiff), western (Bristol) and northern (Manchester). The Crown courts are served by a bench of circuit judges and also by judges of the High Court. According to the Act of 1971, towns with Crown courts are divided up into 'first-tier', 'second-tier' and 'third-tier' centres. In first-tier centres both High Court and circuit judges deal with criminal cases and the High Court judges also hear civil cases. In second-tier centres the High Court and circuit judges only deal with criminal cases, while in third-tier centres there are only circuit judges trying criminal cases.

The bench of circuit judges introduced by the Courts Act is made up from the county court bench, the full-time judges sitting in criminal courts, such as the Old Bailey, and a number of new appointments. The qualification for becoming a circuit judge is to have been a barrister (see p. 70) for ten years, or a Recorder (a part-time judge) for at least five.

Like the Assize courts, Crown courts have a jury of twelve and try indictable, that is the more serious, criminal offences. They also act as appeal courts for people convicted of an offence in the magistrates' court. A person found guilty in a magistrates' court can plead against either conviction or sentence, though if he has pleaded guilty in the lower court he may only appeal against sentence. Appeals from the Crown courts go to the Criminal Division of the Court of Appeal, and in some cases from there to the House of Lords (see p. 50).

Court Procedure Although it is possible for any private citizen to institute criminal proceedings, in practice prosecutions are usually initiated by the police. In serious or contentious cases details are sent to the Director of Public Prosecutions, and it is he who decides whether the case should be proceeded with or not.

Arrests are usually made by police officers – though in law any citizen is empowered to make an arrest – with or without a warrant. Once a person has been arrested and charged with an offence he must be brought before a magistrate within twenty-four hours. (In 1974 this requirement was waived in certain cases relating to 'terrorist' activities.) If this is not possible, and the offence he is alleged to have committed is not serious, the police must release him on bail. Magistrates also have the power to grant bail, though the police may ask for a remand in custody if they suspect that the person may disappear if he is given the opportunity to do so. The decision, however, is left to the magistrate. If a person is freed on bail securities must be given, either by the accused or by someone acting for him. In serious cases the accused is usually remanded until the case against him has been prepared. If a person who is detained considers that this detention is unlawful he can apply for a writ of *habeas corpus* which requires that cause for the detention is shown before the courts.

English criminal law assumes that a person is innocent until he is proved guilty. It is the responsibility of the prosecution to show beyond any reasonable doubt that the defendant has committed the offence of which he is accused. If this cannot be done a verdict of not guilty must be returned. Anyone accused of an offence has the right to employ a legal adviser to present his case, and if he cannot afford to do so he can be provided with legal aid at public expense. All criminal trials, with a few exceptions, such as those involving official secrets, are heard in open court, and the trial is conducted according to strict rules of procedure. All evidence must be given in the presence of the accused, and he, or his counsel, has the right to question all the witnesses. The prosecution may also question the defence witnesses, but they cannot cross-question the accused, unless he decides to go into the witness-box.

As the terms 'prosecution' and 'defence' suggest, an English trial is a contest, in which both sides try to convince the jury that the case which they are presenting is the truth. The judge acts as referee in this contest, and when one side thinks that its opponents are breaking the rules it can appeal to the judge for a ruling. The judge's powers of interference are limited, and he may only intervene in order to check an over-zealous barrister, to advise on a point of law, or to clarify an obscure point. Should he interfere too actively, or show partiality to one side or the other, this may form the basis of an appeal in a higher court.

After the prosecution and defence have concluded their cases, and both sides have presented their final speeches, it is the judge's duty to sum up. In his summing-up speech the judge is expected to outline the case and explain the legal issues involved to the jury. Once the judge has summed up the jury consider their verdict, and in serious cases this can take quite a long time. Should it become apparent that the jury cannot decide on a verdict they will be discharged and a new jury will be selected to hear the trial all over again. However in the vast majority of cases the jury is able to come to a decision. Until 1967 the verdict of the jury had to be unanimous, but since then majority decisions are acceptable, providing that there are not more than two dissentients. If a verdict of not guilty is arrived at, the accused is freed at once. If he is found guilty it is the judge's responsibility to pronounce sentence. He may do this at once, or he may in certain circumstances adjourn the court so that he has time to consider what penalty he should impose. Some judges use the opportunity of passing sentence to deliver a few well-chosen words about the defendant and the crime he has committed, or on occasion about society in general.

Criminal Appeal A person convicted in a magistrates' court can appeal against conviction or sentence to the Crown court. There is also an appeal in some cases to the High Court. Appeals from the Crown courts against conviction or sentence are made to the Court of Appeal (Criminal Division). An appeal against conviction is brought on a point of law – if, for example, it is felt that the judge at the trial has misinterpreted a legal point – or on a question of fact. Appeals against sentence depend on whether the sentence was at the discretion of the judge. The Court of Appeal (Criminal Division) consists of three judges, either Lords Justices of Appeal or judges of the High Court.

They are usually presided over by the Lord Chief Justice or a Justice of Appeal. Appeal from the Court of Appeal to the House of Lords is permitted if it is felt that a point of law of general public importance is involved. A prosecutor or defendant can also appeal to the Lords over a decision of the High Court in a criminal case.

Civil Courts

Civil actions are tried before county courts, before High Court judges sitting in Crown courts, or in the High Court itself. Until they were abolished Assize courts heard civil actions after all the criminal cases on the list had been disposed of. Magistrates' courts also have some limited civil jurisdiction. They can deal with matrimonial proceedings for separation (but not divorce), maintenance orders, adoptions and guardianship.

The county courts were established in 1846 to handle civil cases. At the present time their jurisdiction is limited to actions founded on contract and tort (a private or civil wrong) where the amount claimed is less than £750, equity matters, where the amount involved does not exceed £5,000, and certain actions relating to the recovery of land. Cases outside these limits are heard before High Court judges, sitting either in Crown courts in first-tier centres or in the High Court itself.

The High Court of Justice is divided into the Chancery Division, the Queen's Bench Division and the Family Division. Until the Administration of Justice Act 1970 the third division was Probate, Divorce and Admiralty, strange bed-fellows, but with the common factor that the cases they heard were originally all based on Roman Law. The Family Division of the High Court now deals with all jurisdiction affecting the family: divorce, wardship, guardianship and probate (the ratification of wills). Maritime law is the responsibility of a specially constituted court of the Queen's Bench Division. Although the jurisdiction of the High Court in general covers all civil and some criminal matters, the work is shared out among the different divisions. In the same way, although the sixty-eight puisne judges of the High Court can in theory sit in any division, in practice they are all assigned to a particular one.

The Lord Chancellor (see also p. 51) is President of the Court of Appeal and the Chancery Division. At the head of the Queen's Bench Division is the Lord Chief Justice of England, who is next

to the Lord Chancellor in the legal hierarchy. The most important judge in the Family Division is the President.

High Court judges sit alone when hearing cases of first
instance. Appeals from inferior courts are heard by between
one and three judges nominated by the Lord Chancellor.
Appeals from the High Court and county courts are heard by
the Court of Appeal (Civil Division). The Lord Chancellor, the
Lord Chief Justice, the President of the Family Division and the
Master of the Rolls are *ex officio* members of this; the ordinary
members are fourteen Justices of Appeal.

A case which has been dismissed by the Appeal Court can,
with the permission of the Appeal Court, be taken to the House
of Lords. In a case at which an important legal principle is at
stake the Lords can give permission for an appeal, even if the
Appeal Court has not done so. The judicial function of the
House of Lords is vested in the ten Lords of Appeal in Ordinary,
under the presidency of the Lord Chancellor. The quorum is
three, though it is usual for a group of five or seven law lords
to hear a case.

Most civil disputes are settled by the respective solicitors (see
p. 68) before the case comes to court. When matters cannot be
settled amicably 'out of court', however, expensive litigation
ensues. An action is usually started by the plaintiff (the aggrieved
person) serving a 'writ of summons' on the defendant. This writ
informs the defendant that the plaintiff has a claim against him,
and sets down what that claim is. If the defendant intends to
defend the case by contesting the claim, he 'enters an appearance' by informing the court of his intention, and the relevant
documents are then sent to the court. Anyone not wishing to
go to the trouble and expense of bringing a court case can, if
the other party agrees, have a commercial dispute settled by
arbitration.

Civil actions are for the most part tried by a judge sitting
without a jury. In the case of actions such as defamation (of
character) or false imprisonment, however, either party to the
dispute can request a trial by jury. When a jury is present it
decides not only questions of fact, but also the amount of
damages to be awarded. As juries sometimes award damages
out of all proportion to what is justified it has been suggested
that the responsibility of assessing damages should be given to
the judge, as it is in other civil cases where there is no jury

present. The court is also responsible for deciding who should pay the costs of an action, a question of the greatest importance as litigation is extremely expensive. In general the loser may expect to pay both his own and his opponent's costs, though in many cases the winner finds he has to meet some of his own expenses, even when a costs order is given in his favour.

Because of the high cost of going to law it has been suggested at various times that small claims courts should be introduced to deal with cases involving relatively small amounts of money. There are now three experimental small claims courts in England, where arbitrators try to work out a solution satisfactory to both sides. The system is entirely voluntary, but once both sides have agreed to accept the arbitrator's decision they are bound to do so. The decision is enforceable in the county court. Similar schemes have been introduced in other places.

Other Courts

Coroners' courts, presided over by a lawyer or a doctor, are common law courts which are called when someone dies in suspicious circumstances. The coroner's task is to establish the cause of death, and in cases involving violent death an inquest must be held. Administrative tribunals exist outside the hierarchy of the courts and are set up by Act of Parliament or other statute. Examples of administrative tribunals include the Lands Tribunal, which deals with property values, and rent tribunals, which are concerned with determining fair rents.

THE LEGAL PROFESSION

The legal profession has two branches, barristers (known as advocates in Scotland) and solicitors.

Solicitors

If a person requires legal advice he will go to a solicitor, who for a fee will provide him with the guidance required and advise him on a course of action. Much of the work carried out by a solicitor concerns routine matters, such as buying and selling houses, executing wills and checking documents and contracts, but solicitors are also involved in both criminal and civil cases in courts of law. Normally a person accused of a crime or sued for damages will seek the assistance of a solicitor, who will explain the legal issues involved and take whatever action is necessary on behalf of his client. A solicitor is not permitted to plead in the higher courts, so if the case is to be heard in one of these he must brief a barrister on his client's behalf.

In order to become a solicitor it is necessary to take 'articles of clerkship' (serve an apprenticeship) with an established solicitor for a period of between two and five years. The actual time spent as an articled clerk depends on the educational qualifications of the individual. A university degree in law, for example, provides exemption from certain examinations. However in order to qualify as a solicitor, an articled clerk must pass the Law Society examinations. Once he has done this he becomes a member of the Law Society, the professional organisation for solicitors in England and Wales.

Barristers

The barrister (who has the right of audience before any court or tribunal in England) conducts proceedings in higher courts and also advises on legal problems that have been submitted by solicitors. It is not customary for a prospective client to approach a barrister directly. As we have seen the solicitor acts as intermediary. In order to become a barrister it is necessary to have reached a certain educational standard and to have passed an examination set by the Council of Legal Education. A prospective barrister must gain admittance to one of the four Inns of Court, Lincoln's Inn, the Inner Temple, the Middle Temple or Gray's Inn. Before being 'called to the Bar', i.e. being accepted as a barrister, the candidate must 'keep' eight terms at his Inn. This means that he must dine in the company of his fellow members at the Inn a specified number of times and also pass the Bar examinations. After being 'called' the new barrister is expected to keep another four terms and gain experience under the supervision of a practising barrister.

Should a barrister build up a substantial practice as a 'junior' he may be tempted to 'take silk' and become a 'Queen's Counsel' by applying to the Lord Chancellor for a patent. While this will mean he can charge higher fees than he could as a junior, he is excluded from appearing in less important, but still financially rewarding, cases. However a successful QC can command large fees and he will also enjoy considerable prestige both within the legal fraternity and outside. It is also a logical step up the ladder for an ambitious man, for most of the higher judicial offices are held by Queen's Counsels.

Recently there has been a certain amount of criticism of the legal profession, perhaps the most serious being the charge that by operating a 'closed shop' both solicitors and barristers can claim exorbitant fees. The lawyers reply to charges such as this by pointing out that interpretation of the law is a highly complex business, requiring a great deal of highly skilled work. While this may well be true, in many cases the expense of retaining a solicitor and perhaps a junior barrister and a Queen's Counsel means that the costs of litigation are too high for the average person. This may be a good thing in that it prevents the law courts being jammed with a large number of trivial cases, but it also means that a person with a legitimate case can be deprived of justice because the cost of obtaining this justice is so high. In order to get over some of the difficulties of the high cost of going to law, provision has been made for legal aid to be granted in both civil and criminal cases. Legal aid in criminal cases is usually granted at the discretion of the court, and in most cases the defendant will be expected to make some contribution towards the cost of his lawyers. In civil cases only applicants with very low incomes qualify for free legal aid. In 1972 a new scheme was announced under which people with low incomes could obtain the services of a solicitor up to the value of £25.

Judges
The English judiciary prides itself on its impartiality and its freedom from political involvement. Judges are appointed by the Lord Chancellor, himself the senior judge in the country and head of the legal profession, from the senior members of the Bar (or Recorders from Crown courts) and they are non-political appointments. On a number of occasions judges have made legal decisions that have proved acutely embarrassing to the government of the day, for Acts of Parliament that have been ambiguously drafted may be interpreted by the courts in a manner far different from that intended by legislators.

Once a judge has been appointed it is virtually impossible to unseat him. The only way to remove a member of the bench is by a petition to Parliament. As there is no official retiring age for judges there is a danger that some of them may go on exercising their judicial functions their when intellectual powers have begun to decline. There is also a tendency for some of them to take advantage of their position to pontificate on what they consider to be the evils of modern society. This has been particularly true in divorce cases where the presiding judge may well take it upon himself to deliver a homily about married life or the morals of the individuals involved in the case.

There has also been criticism of the fact that judges are responsible for passing sentences even when they have very little knowledge of the defendant's background, or of the nature of the punishment they are prescribing. As a judge is trained solely as a lawyer he may have little knowledge of psychology or criminology, and may indeed be rather critical when experts in these sciences appear in his court as witnesses.

As we have seen, when a barrister 'takes silk' he becomes a Queen's Counsel, which gives him the right to use the letters QC after his name, for example Peter Brown QC. Should he then be selected as a 'circuit judge' he will be known as 'His Honour Judge Brown'. If, on the other hand, he becomes a judge in the High Court, he will be referred to as 'The Honourable Mr Justice Brown', and he will also be knighted. If he is promoted to the Appeal Court he will be addressed as 'Lord Justice Brown' (although he is not a member of the peerage) or the 'Right Honourable Sir Peter Brown'. As a 'Lord of Appeal in Ordinary' he would become a life peer with a seat in the Lords and the title of 'The Right Honourable Lord Brown'.

THE JURY

The modern jury in England and Wales consists of twelve men or women, between the ages of eighteen and sixty-five. They have the responsibility of deciding whether their fellow citizen who is on trial is innocent or guilty of the offence of which he is accused. After hearing all the evidence in the case the jury listen to the judge's summing up, and then withdraw to consider their verdict. Until recently juries had to be unanimous in their verdicts, but the law now allows for majority verdicts, provided there are no more than two dissentients in a jury of twelve. Should a jury be unable to agree a new trial must be held, though in practice this rarely happens. Juries serve in both criminal and civil courts, deciding questions of fact, and in the case of the former, the damages that should be paid to the injured party. Juries do not fix penalties, though in the days when the death penalty was still in force for murder the jury might make a plea for leniency for someone who was likely to be condemned to death as a result of a verdict of 'guilty'.

There are those who claim that the whole concept of the jury is out of date, and that trial by jury should be replaced by trial by experts, as in fact happens in the civil cases where a judge sits alone. Critics of the jury system point to the extravagant damages that juries sometimes award in civil cases. They also claim that juries are subject to prejudices to such an extent that many verdicts are decided almost before the first evidence is presented, particularly in cases involving crimes against the person. The juryman is of course supposed to be completely impartial and to have no advance knowledge of the case, but it is very difficult to secure these conditions. Another criticism of juries is that it is easy for organised criminal gangs to bribe or threaten jurors in order to influence their verdicts. In the days when unanimous verdicts were required it was only necessary for one member of the jury to be intimidated to make it impossible to obtain a verdict.

SCOTLAND

As Scotland was an independent kingdom until 1707 its legal system differs from that of England and Wales in a number of respects. However since the early eighteenth century many of the statutes introduced by Parliament also apply to Scotland, which means that in many cases Scottish law is in line with that of England and Wales. Nevertheless differences of organisation and procedure are still marked, while sometimes a law that exists in England and Wales may not apply in Scotland and vice versa.

The Scottish Courts
The courts of summary jurisdiction in Scotland are the burgh (or police) courts, presided over by town councillors, and the Justice of the Peace courts, which are found outside urban areas and are presided over by judges, sitting in their capacity as Justices of the Peace. Sheriff courts, which serve counties or

combinations of counties known as 'sheriffdoms', hear both civil and criminal cases. The supreme criminal court of first instance (i.e. the court that tries and sentences an offender) is the High Court of Judiciary. Cases in the High Court are heard by the Lord Justice General, the Lord Justice Clerk or one of the Lords Commissioner of Justiciary. The court is based in Edinburgh, but the judges also go on circuit. Appeals in criminal cases are made to the High Court. There is no appeal to the House of Lords.

The main courts of civil jurisdiction in Scotland are the sheriff courts, while the highest civil court is the Court of Session. The sheriff courts can handle virtually all cases, actions being heard by the sheriff. Appeals can be made to the Sheriff-Principal (the leading sheriff in a sheriffdom) or to the Court of Session. The Court of Session has two parts, an Outer and an Inner House, the former being a court of first instance, the latter mainly an appeal court. From the Inner House an appeal can be made to the House of Lords.

THE POLICE

In 1957 there were 126 police forces in England and Wales and 20 in Scotland. They ranged in size from the Metropolitan Police Force, responsible for policing Greater London, which had 16,419 officers, to one of the Scottish forces which had 16. During the sixties, largely as a result of recommendations made by the Royal Commission on the Police which reported in 1962, a large number of amalgamations took place. In 1974 there were 47 police forces in England and Wales, with an average strength outside London of 1,800, and 20 in Scotland, most of which were smaller in size.

The oldest police force in the country is the Metropolitan Police, founded by Sir Robert Peel, then Home Secretary, in 1829. Peel's men were responsible for maintaining order in the capital, and though distrusted and reviled at first, they soon became so successful that they were imitated in other parts of the country. Whereas the Metropolitan Police Force was responsible to the Home Secretary, police forces in other areas were established by local bodies. Although proposals have been made at times that a national force should be set up, there has been little support for the idea from either police or public. At the present time each local force is maintained by a police authority, made up of representatives of the councils covered by the force, and local magistrates. It is the responsibility of the police authority to appoint a chief constable and his immediate subordinates and to provide the equipment to enable the police to carry out their duties. The Home Secretary in England and Wales and the Secretary of State for Scotland exercise a certain amount of control over police forces, by having the final say in the appointment of chief constables and making general regulations covering administration, pay and terms of service. They also appoint the chief inspectors of constabulary, who with their deputies are responsible for inspecting the forces throughout the country (outside London), reporting back to the appropriate Secretary of State.

5

The Welfare State

It was not until relatively recently that society felt that it had an obligation to provide protection for those of its members who were sick, old, unemployed or suffering from some other form of deprivation or hardship. During the Middle Ages the feudal system in rural areas and the 'guilds' in the towns provided some degree of protection. In country districts every man had an overlord who looked after the interests of his underlings, though, of course, the feudal system was heavily weighted in favour of the upper classes. The rights of serfs were either very limited or nonexistent. In towns the guilds, which were established to protect the standards of certain trades and to regulate admission to the ranks of skilled craftsmen, also gave assistance to members who were in difficulties. For the destitute and landless there was little or no provision; they were dependent on alms from those who were more fortunate than they, or from the monasteries and convents.

During Tudor times some attempts were made to deal with the problem of the poor and unemployed. At the end of Elizabeth I's reign a Poor Law was passed, and this was to remain the backbone of social legislation in England until 1834, when the Poor Law Amendment Act was introduced. The Poor Law was, as it was intended to be, a harsh Act, designed as much as anything to discourage people from relying on public funds. The fact that the Poor Law remained basically unchanged for over two hundred years is not a testimony to its humanity and effectiveness – rather it shows the attitude of the times. In the opinion of most leading politicians, industrialists, landowners and churchmen, it was not the business of the government to interfere with the running of factories and mines or the building of houses. According to this attitude poverty was not the result of low wages, but of fecklessness and a lack of incentive to work. So industrialists of the eighteenth and early nineteenth centuries continued to build insanitary houses for their workers, forced them to work long hours in shocking conditions and paid them minimal wages. In all this they were aided and abetted by Governments which refused to permit working men to organise and to form trade unions to protest against their conditions.

Although a number of important and beneficial reforms were introduced during the first decade of the nineteenth century, they were conceived in a paternalistic manner, while the attitude that poverty was the fault of the poor was still very much in evidence. Nowhere is this more clearly seen than in the Poor Law Amendment Act of 1834, which set up workhouses in place of the 'outdoor relief' introduced by the Elizabethan Poor Law. The theory behind the workhouses was that conditions inside their walls should be more unpleasant than any work available outside, thereby discouraging all but the completely destitute from entering the institution. The harsh regime of the workhouse was designed to stop able-bodied but lazy men from going on relief, but in practice all the inmates had to suffer the strict rules, which led to the separation of families, inadequate food (Oliver Twist was not the only one who wanted more) and insanitary conditions. It is not surprising that before long the workhouse came to be regarded with fear and loathing by the poor, to be avoided at all costs.

Because of the failure of the state to provide security against sickness or unemployment, except in the form of the workhouse, by the middle of the nineteenth century a number of Friendly Societies had been formed. These societies provided financial assistance and medical care in cases of sickness and also a funeral grant so that members who died could avoid the indignity of a pauper burial.

Another area where the authorities were slow to act was public health. In spite of the fact that towns were increasing in size at a prodigious rate at the end of the eighteenth and beginning of the nineteenth centuries, there were few regulations governing building standards. The result was that slums of 'back-to-back' houses, without proper drainage or ventilation, became commonplace in many industrial cities. Cramped living conditions and indifference to proper methods of rubbish and sewage disposal led to a number of serious outbreaks of infectious disease during the nineteenth century, for example, cholera in 1831–32 and 1848–9, and smallpox in 1881. Following the first cholera epidemic a number of towns established boards of health, but it was not until the Public Health Act of 1848 that a national General Board of Health was set up. In 1875 a second Public Health Act introduced a nation-wide system of public health, under the control of the Local Government Board. In the same year an Act was passed which provided for the clearance of slum districts, while a number of other Acts of the seventies and eighties relating to education, trade unions and housing showed that the government was belatedly recognising that it had responsibilities towards the community as a whole.

By the end of the nineteenth century there were a number of Acts providing protection from the worst excesses of the industrial system. However it should be stressed that many of the Acts had only been accepted after a long and bitter struggle both inside and outside Parliament. The social legislation of the nineteenth century was in most cases the work of a few men and women who had to struggle against the indifference, and frequently the hostility, of parliamentarians of both parties.

Between 1906 and 1914 the Liberal Party was instrumental in introducing a far-reaching programme of social reform. Here again the question of motives arises. Opinions differ as to how far the Liberals were really interested in improving the welfare of the less well-off members of society, and how far they were continuing the paternalism of the previous century. Whatever the motives behind the reforms introduced by the Liberal administration that held office in the years before the First World War, they were to have considerable impact on the country. Particularly important were the 1908 Old Age Pensions Act and the National Insurance Act of 1911. Other measures included the setting up of labour exchanges, legislation to improve the position of trade unionists and a minimum wage for coal miners. Reforms affecting education covered the provision of school meals and a medical service for schoolchildren.

Despite reforms such as these, up until the First World War the government intervened very little in the life of the average citizen. Many people were totally unaffected by the welfare legislation just described, while some still regarded the provision of aid to the unemployed and sick as aiding and abetting laziness and dishonesty. During the war the government became much more involved in the personal life of citizens, as virtually the whole country was mobilised to meet the threat of total war.

Regulations were introduced which affected the whole population, including the Defence of the Realm Act, which gave the government powers that were almost dictatorial in the interests of safeguarding the country and winning the war.

After the war the state's powers of intervention were cut back to some extent, but there was no return to the conditions of 1914. For some, Lloyd George's promises to build a country 'fit for heroes to live in' implied that a far-reaching programme of social reform would be undertaken; but in spite of a widening of the scope of the National Insurance Act, and legislation to build more houses, developments during the inter-war years were disappointing. Indeed the economic crises of the twenties and thirties showed only too clearly that the action taken to provide unemployment benefits was of limited value when it was a question of dealing with two or three million workers without jobs. Housing was provided by local councils at cheap rents that were subsidised by the state, but even so demand outstripped supply, and housing conditions in many industrial cities were extremely poor at this time.

It was during the Second World War that the blueprint for the welfare state was produced by a committee under the chairmanship of Sir William Beveridge. The Beveridge Report, published in 1942, outlined a comprehensive scheme of social security, designed, as Beveridge said, to attack want, disease, ignorance, squalor and idleness. The Beveridge plan proposed a complete break with the old Poor Law outlook which was still prevalent in British welfare circles, and the substitution of an entirely new concept. The plan was 'first and foremost a plan of insurance', towards which individuals paid a contribution, and from which they received benefits when needed, as of right. The plan also provided for child allowances, a national health service and an end to mass unemployment. There was a tremendous public response to the plan, and in 1944 a draft Bill was published. A Ministry of National Insurance was set up in the same year. In June 1945 Churchill's caretaker Government passed a Family Allowance Act, but as it was defeated at the general election in October it was unable to follow this up with further legislation.

The Labour Party had accepted the main principles of the Beveridge report shortly after it was published and after coming to power they lost little time in introducing the necessary legislation. The Family Allowances Act already mentioned came into effect in August 1946 and provided a weekly allowance of 5 shillings (25p) for every child except the first. The allowance was available to all, but as it was taxable it meant that people with larger incomes received little or no benefit. By 1975 the family allowance had risen to £1.50, and from 1977 it is to be paid for all children.

The National Insurance (Industrial Injuries) Act provided compensation for those injured at work, but was to a large extent overshadowed by the main National Insurance Act which became law in 1946. By the terms of this Act the entire adult population, that is everybody between the school-leaving age of fifteen and the retirement age of sixty-five, was compulsorily insured for sickness benefit, unemployment benefit, retirement pension, widow's pension, maternity grants and allowances, and death grants. As in the case of the 1911 Act, contributions came from employee, employer (except of course in the case of self-employed and non-employed persons) and the state. But the contributions were to be administered by the recently established Ministry of National Insurance (now the Department of Health and Social Security), not by Friendly Societies and insurance companies as previously.

The National Health Act was also passed in 1946, though it did not begin to operate until July 1948. Its aim was to provide the nation with a complete range of medical services, including those of specialists, dentists and hospital staff, as far as possible without charge to the patient. The cost of the National Health Service (the NHS) was to be met out of general taxation, while a proportion of the receipts from national insurance would also contribute towards its upkeep. The Act had far-reaching implications, for by providing, or seeking to provide, a comprehensive service for every member of the community, it completely changed the structure of medical care in the United Kingdom.

Hospitals which had previously been administered by local authorities or voluntary societies were brought under the control of fourteen regional hospital boards in England and Wales. In Scotland and Northern Ireland complementary but distinct National Health Acts established hospital boards, five in the former and one in the latter area. The day-to-day running of hospitals was made the responsibility of hospital management committees, with overall control being exercised by the Minister of Health. The original Bill had proposed that doctors should come under the control of local authorities, but the doctors' professional organisation, the British Medical Association, protested so violently about this idea that executive councils were established instead. The 138 councils were responsible under the Ministry of Health for keeping records, paying doctors and dentists for their services and for overseeing the running of the 'Family Practitioner Services' at the local level. The third main division of the NHS was the local health services, which provided facilities for the maintenance of health. These local health services included home nursing, child welfare, health visiting and ambulances.

A year after the National Health Service was introduced it covered 95 per cent of the population and cost almost £400 million a year to run. By the mid-seventies the cost of running the Health Service had risen to over £3,000 million a year.

Although when the Health Service was introduced it was intended that treatment and medicines would be provided without extra charge to patients, later some charges were introduced for medicines. This was bitterly opposed by the left wing of the Labour Party, who felt that the basic concept of the NHS was being undermined. At the present time a charge is made for medicines and some forms of treatment, for example dental care, but certain categories of patient, such as pregnant women, are exempt from charges. In cases of hardship or prolonged illness, medicines are free.

The Poor Law was finally brought to an end legally in 1948, though in practice it had ceased to function during the 1930s when the number of unemployed was so great that the guardians could not meet their responsibilities. The National Assistance Act of 1948 set up the National Assistance Board which was designed to aid those in need. Basic rates of assistance were laid down by the national government, though individual offices were given discretionary powers.

THE WELFARE STATE TODAY

The National Health Service

The National Health Service has come in for considerable criticism during its few decades of existence. In the opinion of many people its objectives are too ambitious for the limited funds that are available, and the press and other media are constantly forecasting its imminent collapse. Nor are criticisms confined to those outside the Health Service: doctors, nurses, radiographers and others who work in hospitals and elsewhere have on many occasions expressed their dissatisfaction with the terms of service – particularly rates of pay, level of staffing and the running of the NHS. However while many of these criticisms are undoubtedly founded on fact it does not necessarily follow that the NHS has been a failure. Indeed it can be argued that far from failing the Health Service has been too successful, in that the provision of a wide range of health services at little or no cost has increased consumer demand. Those who previously did not get medical attention are now receiving it and many people who before 1948 would have died are now receiving treatment and being cured.

Recently there have been a number of clashes between the government and certain sectors of the medical profession on the question of private treatment in National Health Service hospitals. The Department of Health and Social Security has announced that it intends to phase out the system whereby a certain number of 'pay beds' (i.e. beds for the use of 'private' or paying patients) are available, but many doctors are opposed to this move. There have also been renewed protests – some of which have included industrial action such as refusing to work overtime – over pay and conditions in the health service by doctors, nurses and auxiliary staff.

There are some 25,000 general practitioners (family doctors) in Great Britain, each with an average of 2,400 patients (the maximum permitted is 3,500). There are about 30,000 medical staff in hospitals, over 10,000 of whom are consultants or senior doctors, and some 350,000 nurses. The NHS has about 2,700 hospitals with a total of 505,000 beds. Dentists belonging to the National Health Service number 12,500.

Since April 1974, when the National Health Service Re-organisation Act took effect, the NHS has been administered as a single unified service. In place of the regional hospital boards, the executive councils and the personal health services run by local authorities there are in England three levels of planning: regional, area and the central Department. The Secretary of State for Health and Social Security has overall responsibility for policy and for supervising the regional and area authorities. There are fourteen regional health authorities (RHAs), each of which incorporates a university medical school. Members of the RHA are appointed by the Secretary of State in consultation with interested organisations such as the universities and local authorities. It is the responsibility of the regional authority to act as a link between the Secretary of State and the area authorities, and also to oversee the work done in the region as a whole and in each of the areas for which it is responsible. The boundaries of the area health authorities (AHAs) are for the most part the same as for the major local government authorities which came into being in April 1974. There are ninety AHAs in England (Wales has twelve AHAs and Scotland fifteen health boards which perform similar functions; there are no RHAs outside England). The chairman of each AHA is appointed by the Secretary of State, while the remaining members are appointed by the local authorities, the local university and the RHA. A number of the members of the authority are professionals, e.g. doctors and nurses, the others laymen. The AHA is responsible for running the health services in the area for which it is responsible, Doctors, dentists, opticians, pharmacists and others offering professional services remain as independent contractors. In place of the executive councils each AHA has a Family Practitioner Committee consisting of thirty members. Half the committee members are appointed by the interested professions, eleven by the AHA and four by the local authority.

The AHA is the body that puts the Health Service into effect, as it is responsible for deciding what the needs of the area are and for meeting these needs. In addition to providing medical staff the AHAs also ensure that there are adequate services to back up the work done in the surgeries and hospitals. The AHA is divided into districts, each of which has a population of between 200,000 and 500,000. The number of districts is decided by the AHA. While some areas contain only one district, others that are more populous may have up to five.

In 1970 the Local Authority Social Services Act enabled county councils, county boroughs and London boroughs to set up social services departments to integrate the personal social services. Following local government reorganisation these are administered by the county and metropolitan county councils.

The welfare of young people, juvenile offenders, the physically handicapped, the mentally ill, the elderly and the homeless are all the concern of the local authority social services departments. The facilities provided by the NHS and those of the local authorities are intended to complement each other.

National Insurance Payments and Benefits

Every working person over the minimum school-leaving age (sixteen) must make a weekly national insurance contribution; contributions are also made by the employer. The following are the main benefits available under the national insurance scheme: unemployment benefit, paid after three days out of work and continued for up to twelve months; sickness benefit, which is paid as long as incapacity for work continues; invalidity benefit, which is paid after sickness benefit has been paid for twenty-eight weeks; maternity benefit, a grant and an allowance if the mother has been working; and retirement pension, payable to men over sixty-five and women over sixty who have stopped working. Widow's benefits, child's special allowance and a death grant are also included in the scheme. Industrial injuries benefits are paid to employees injured at work or suffering from industrial diseases.

In 1966 the National Assistance Board, which was set up in 1948, was replaced by the Supplementary Benefits Commission. Supplementary benefits are payable to people who are not in full-time work and whose resources are insufficient to meet their needs. Many of those who receive supplementary benefits are already getting national insurance benefit; a very large proportion of them are old age pensioners, while others are unemployed or sick. There are also people who for one reason or another do not qualify for national insurance benefits, and for whom the supplementary benefit is the main source of income. The Commission is responsible for deciding who is entitled to receive supplementary benefit, and also at what rate it should be paid. In 1970 the Family Income Supplement Act made the Supplementary Benefits Commission responsible for paying Family Income Supplement to families with very low incomes. Considerable anxiety has been aroused by the fact that supplementary benefit was not payable to families where the breadwinner was in full-time employment, even though the income of the family was below the minimum level provided by the supplementary benefit scheme.

The standard weekly flat-rate pension is £13.30 and £21.20 for a married couple. In addition there is the graduated pensions scheme that was started in 1961. However employees whose job provides them with a pension can contract out of the graduated scheme, and pay a reduced contribution.

HOUSING

For the average Englishman (and his cousins elsewhere in the British Isles) the only real home is a house. It is estimated that over 80 per cent of the population of Britain live in houses or bungalows, the remainder in flats or maisonettes. A house can be detached, semi-detached or in a terrace, but ideally should stand in its own garden and have both a front and a back door. Although the bungalow has become increasingly popular in recent years, the traditional British house has two storeys, the bottom one containing the living rooms (or in the language of the estate agent the 'reception rooms'), and kitchen, and the upper floor the bedrooms and bathroom. The average house built in this century has two living rooms and two or three bedrooms, and there is often storage space in the form of a pantry (for food) or cupboards. The commonest building material is brick, though many of the houses built in the last three decades use prefabricated techniques, employing concrete, plastics and other modern materials.

It is estimated that there are over nineteen million dwellings in the United Kingdom. About half of these are owner-occupied, 30 per cent are rented from local authorities, while the remainder are rented from private landlords. (An estimated 200,000 families, about 1 per cent of the population, have two homes.) As few people have sufficient money to buy a house outright, the usual procedure is to take a loan, in the form of a mortgage from a building society or other financial institution, or a local authority. This long-term loan, which is usually paid back over a period of twenty or twenty-five years, is given at a comparatively low rate of interest, though recently the rise in interest rates has been causing considerable concern. In 1964 the standard rate was 6 per cent, in 1974 this had risen to 11 per cent, and there were fears that it would go even higher. The four hundred or so building societies in Britain provide the finance for the purchase of some 90 per cent of the houses built in the country. At the beginning of the seventies house prices rose spectacularly. During the 1960s the price of houses had risen on average by 6.6 per cent each year; in 1971 prices increased by 22.1 per cent, while in 1972 some houses doubled in value in a matter of months. During the first three months of 1973 the price of houses rose by 10 per cent, with new houses selling at an average price of £9,483, about £3,000 more than in the first three months of 1972. In July 1973 it was announced that the average price of a new house mortgaged with a building society had gone up by 87 per cent between the second quarter of 1970 and the first quarter of 1973. This dramatic rise in house prices has meant that it has become very difficult for low-paid workers and those trying to get a first mortgage to raise money for a house of their own. During the first three months of 1973 building societies lent £967 million, £32 million more than in the same months of 1972, but the money financed 11,000 fewer house purchases. Since 1973 the increase in house prices has slowed down as building society funds have been restricted.

The amount of money advanced by building societies depends largely on the age of the house and the salary of the prospective borrower (and of course the funds the society has at its disposal). It is possible to get a mortgage of 90 per cent, or even more, on a new house, but the amount lent on an older property would not normally be so high.

Local authorities are also entitled to lend money for house purchase, but they are usually expected to pay special attention to people who are unable to obtain finance from other sources. Mortgage interest payments are given tax relief. At the beginning of the seventies a new mortgage scheme (the option mortgage scheme) was introduced, at a lower rate of interest, but without tax relief, to assist those with lower incomes.

About 39 per cent of Britain's housing stock has been built since the Second World War, that is, about seven million dwellings. Many older houses, particularly those in urban areas, are in bad condition, and there is an urgent need to redevelop slum and semi-slum areas, where there is overcrowding and a lack of essential facilities. Although over 360,000 dwellings are being built each year, nearly half of them by public authorities, it is estimated that over four million dwellings have inadequate amenities or require substantial repairs, while many should be condemned as they are unfit for human habitation. The lack o adequate housing has been a problem for many years, and is made worse by the fact that many of the worst houses are privately owned by landlords who have little incentive to provide improved conditions for their tenants. Until 1957 rents were controlled, but in that year a Rent Act was passed which permitted rents to rise at the same rate as prices. The declared aim behind this Act was to make it financially attractive for people to buy property for renting. It was hoped that more dwellings would thus become available and the housing shortage would be eased. However the Act introduced a number of new problems, one of which was that while 'sitting tenants' were permitted to retain their tenancies without an increase in rent, new tenants could be charged at a higher rate. This situation meant that people whose interest lay in making money, rather than helping with the housing problem, could make a lucrative business out of buying up large houses with several 'sitting tenants' cheaply, and then forcing these tenants out. The house, minus tenants, could then be sold at a considerable profit. In 1965 a further Rent Act was introduced, restoring security of tenure for tenants and providing strong penalties for harassment. The basis of the new Act was a 'regulated tenancy', fixed at a 'fair rent' by a rent officer. Should the landlord or tenant object to the rent officer's decision, the case could go to the rent assessment committee for consideration. Once a rent had been fixed it would remain in force for three years. In 1974 the provisions of the Rent Act were extended to include furnished accommodation.

It might appear that the answer to profiteering by landlords is for local authorities to provide cheap housing. However, although there are some six million publicly-owned dwellings (council houses), demand usually exceeds supply. Most local authorities, particularly those in large towns where the need is greatest, have long waiting lists. Preference is usually given to large families, or those living in unsuitable or overcrowded conditions, but in some areas it seems that only too often those who are in the greatest need are unable to get the housing they require.

Housing societies, which build dwellings for co-ownership or to let, have become widespread following the establishment of the Housing Corporation in 1964. It is estimated that housing societies and associations own about 170,000 houses in England

and Wales. Housing societies are financed by building societies and the Housing Corporation, each of which provides 50 per cent of the money needed for building.

In spite of the fact that the people of Britain are better housed today than at any other time in their history, the problem of housing is still a major one. An estimated 37 per cent of the housing stock was built before 1919. While much of this is in good condition, particularly in country areas where possession of an old (but modernised) country cottage is regarded as a status symbol, and in residential suburbs, there are many urban areas where bad conditions still exist. There are also a depressingly large number of people who do not have homes of any kind, and who have to rely on hostels provided by local authorities, many of which are reminiscent of the workhouses of the last century. One body that has been actively fighting poor housing conditions and the problems of the homeless is Shelter, which has branches in many large towns. There are many people who feel that the provision of housing is not the responsibility of the state or local authorities, and that individuals should make their own arrangements. However, as we have seen it is difficult for those with low salaries to qualify for a building society mortgage, unless they can produce a large deposit from their savings. Housing is always one of the most important issues in elections, at both local and national level. There is little doubt that with the very large increases in the price of houses in recent years the problem will continue to be a pressing one.

6

Education

The English education system has always tended to resemble a handicap race. However, whereas in the usual form of handicap race the aim is to give all competitors an equal chance of winning by placing some impediment on those who have an advantage, the aim of the English school system seems to be to give those who have an advantage an even greater one.

The first English schools were founded by the Church in the sixth century, to train boys for the priesthood, and the Church was to retain a virtual monopoly of education for many centuries. During the Middle Ages most of the schools that existed were attached to cathedrals, monasteries or collegiate churches, though they were sometimes supplemented by establishments founded and endowed by rich burgesses for the education of their sons. The state played virtually no part in education. Although individual monarchs could follow the example of Alfred the Great and establish particular institutions, as Henry VI did in the case of Eton, the state accepted no responsibility for either organising or financing any educational system. During Tudor times a number of schools were established; Edward VI founded some dozen schools, still known as King Edward VI Grammar Schools, while a number of others opened their doors in Elizabeth I's reign.

Education was the prerogative of the rich. Although scholarships existed for 'poor and needy' boys who showed an aptitude for learning, there were not nearly enough of them to provide places for all those having this qualification. If a child did not attend school he might pick up the rudiments of reading and writing from a parent, relative or neighbour, but in many cases people were illiterate for life. A number of the giants of the Industrial Revolution had received little or no formal education; James Brindley, the great canal engineer, taught himself to write in order to be able to keep his notebooks up to date, while the older Stephenson, of 'Rocket' fame, was illiterate to manhood.

During the late eighteenth century a considerable number of 'industrial schools' and 'Sunday schools' were established by industrialists and philanthropists. These institutions were intended to provide a basic education for the working class, or at least what their founders considered to be a basic education. The men who set up these schools were not particularly concerned about training future Brindleys and Stephensons to read plans and technical works; they were more anxious to ensure that their workers could read the Bible. Thus the main emphasis was to provide a man or child with enough reading knowledge to stumble through the scriptures, while arithmetic, writing and other potentially dangerous subjects were practically ignored. One of the great problems of these early schools was a shortage of trained teachers, for frequently parents as well as children crowded into the classrooms.

At the beginning of the nineteenth century such elementary schools as existed were financed either by private individuals or the churches. Local authorities were empowered to make grants towards education from the rates if they saw fit to do so, but by no means all of them did. The Church of England no longer had the monopoly of education it had enjoyed in earlier times, and frequently found itself in conflict with non-conformists over which church should have the right to provide education in a particular area. At times the issue became so heated, and the opponents so involved in questions of principle, that the children were completely forgotten and remained uneducated.

If the churches wanted to fight over the right to educate the young, the state for its part seemed indifferent. This aloofness was to continue until 1833, when Parliament made a grant of £20,000 for the provision of 'school houses'. Although this grant could hardly be described as generous, it did mark the beginning of the state's involvement in education, which was to increase throughout the century, culminating in the Education Act of 1870. This Act, often known as the Forster Act after the man who piloted it through Parliament, established some 300 school boards throughout the country which were empowered to provide schools for elementary education in their respective areas. By the end of the decade a national system of education had been established, providing free compulsory education for all children between the ages of five and ten (fourteen by 1900).

Although elementary education for all had been achieved, secondary education was still the privilege of those who were able to pay for it. The nineteenth century saw a revival of the ancient secondary schools, many of which received new endowments, enabling them to expand and enlarge their intake of pupils – fee-paying, of course. In addition to the revival of the old-established schools, many new ones were founded. Like their predecessors, they provided an exclusive education, based on the classics, for members of the middle and upper classes. The Victorian public school – 'public' then, as now, meant 'private' – was, however, much more than mere bricks and mortar. It quickly became the training ground for the men who were to rule Britain and the Empire. At the beginning of the century most of the public schools were in a bad way. Neither the masters nor the pupils seemed to have much interest in education, while discipline was so bad that on one occasion the military were called in to suppress a riot at one of the best-known schools. Under the influence of such men as Samuel Butler and Thomas Arnold, however, things began to change. Butler revised the syllabus at his school, Shrewsbury, placing an emphasis on a liberal education; while at Rugby Arnold laid the foundations of the public schools' role as institutions where boys were trained to be Christian gentlemen. A Royal Commission appointed to report on seven of the most prestigious schools in 1864 found much to be commended in them, and as a result the position of the public schools was confirmed by the Public Schools Act of 1868.

It was not until the beginning of the twentieth century that an opportunity was provided for children whose parents could not afford heavy school fees to benefit from secondary education. Under the terms of the 1902 Education Act, 25 per cent of the places in secondary schools, excluding public schools, were reserved for scholarship pupils. In 1918 the Fisher Education Act increased the number of secondary schools, but the demand for places still exceeded the supply, and the position did not improve much before the 1940s. But a number of reports had been commissioned between the two world wars, and in 1944 a new Education Act was passed, which reorganised secondary education in England and Wales.

One of the reforms effected by the 1944 (Butler) Act, was that the President of the Board of Education was replaced by a Minister of Education. This minister was expected to 'promote the education of the people of England and Wales . . . and to secure the effective execution by local authorities . . . of the national policy for providing a varied and comprehensive educational service in every area'. This effectively meant that guidelines were drawn up by the ministry, while the individual education authorities decided what form education would take in their area. The Act stipulated that education would be divided into three stages: primary, from five to twelve; secondary, over twelve to under nineteen; and further – post-school. The school-leaving age was fixed at fifteen, with the intention of raising it to sixteen when facilities became available. Other important clauses of the Act dealt with the welfare role of local authorities in relation to education, a standardised scale of payment for all teachers employed by local authorities, and a system of inspection for independent schools (those outside the state system).

The 1944 Act defined two kinds of state schools, county and voluntary. The former were provided and maintained by the local authority, while the latter were schools that had been originally founded by the churches. Voluntary schools, the vast majority of which are primary schools, are divided into three categories: 'controlled', 'aided' and 'special agreement'. The distinction between the different categories depends largely on the amount of financial assistance given by the local authority, and the powers the authority and the religious body have over appointing certain members of staff.

The Act paved the way for two kinds of secondary school, the grammar school and the secondary modern school. Some areas had a third type, the secondary technical school, while in some areas the local education authority gained ministry approval for more individual schemes. In Anglesey, in North Wales, for example, a comprehensive system, in which all pupils of secondary school age went to the same kind of school, was instituted. For the majority of pupils, however, the existence of two different kinds of school meant a choice, and in most cases the choice was made on the basis of examination results. The decisive examination, known as the 11-plus, was taken in the last year at the primary school, and its intention was to distinguish between academic and non-academic children. Those who did well in the intelligence and other tests that made up the examination passed, and went to grammar schools, while those who failed went to secondary modern schools, where they received a less academic type of education. It was the intention of those who had framed the 1944 Act that there should be 'parity of esteem' between the different kinds of secondary school, that is that the grammar schools should not be considered 'better' in any way than the other schools. However good the intentions of the men and women responsible for the Act, they seem to have failed to take into account the pressures of the postwar social system, and to have totally miscalculated the reactions of parents, teachers and children.

The grammar schools prepared children for the General Certificate of Education examinations at Ordinary and Advanced level, which are the qualifications for entry to higher education and the professions. In secondary modern schools, on the other hand, the emphasis was on practical education, leading to skilled or unskilled jobs. It is not surprising therefore that the secondary modern pupil felt himself inferior to the child who went to the grammar school. He qualified for his school by failing an examination, and then found that he was unable to take the later examinations he would need to pass if he wanted to continue into higher education. Pressure from parents and teachers forced many secondary modern schools to introduce courses leading to GCE examinations, and before long the secondary modern schools in many areas had become imitation grammar schools.

It was this state of affairs, together with growing scepticism about the ability of the 11-plus examination to predict the long-term intellectual ability of the child, that led many educationalists to press for the introduction of comprehensive schools. These were to be non-selective and would provide courses for children of all levels of ability. In spite of the fact that the Labour Government of 1945–51 had accepted the 1944 Act with its principle of selection, during the fifties attitudes changed, and when the Labour Party returned to power in 1964 it announced that it would introduce a system of comprehensive schools throughout the country.

In 1965 the Secretary of State sent out a circular (Circular 10/65) which invited all local authorities to submit plans for the introduction of comprehensive education. By the beginning of 1970, most of the 163 local education authorities had done so, though some had refused, presumably for political reasons. In February 1970, therefore, the Secretary of State for Education introduced a Bill 'to impose on local authorities a duty to plan for and to achieve a system of comprehensive secondary education'. During the debate on the Bill the Conservative spokesman on education said that if it was passed the Conservatives would repeal it when they returned to power. This, however, proved unnecessary as the Bill did not go through before the 1970 general election. One of the first actions of the incoming Conservative Secretary of State was to withdraw Circular 10/65, and replace it with Circular 10/70. The new circular stated that the Government felt it was wrong to impose a uniform pattern of secondary education by legislation, and that local authorities should be free to choose the kind of secondary education they considered was best fitted to local needs. In most cases the authorities who had made considerable progress along the road to comprehensive schools decided to continue with their policy. Others who, for one reason or another, had been slower in getting started, announced that they would retain selection. In February 1974, however, a Labour government was once again returned to power and the new Secretary of State for Education announced that it was Labour policy to introduce a fully comprehensive system in England and Wales, if necessary by legislation. There were in the mid-seventies about 1,800 comprehensive schools, 1,900 secondary modern schools and just under 1,000 grammar schools in the state sector in England and Wales. At the end of 1975 the Government gave details of a Bill that would require all local authorities to submit plans for the introduction of comprehensive schools.

One of the reasons for the complexity of the English education system is that the government is unwilling to intervene directly in education at the local level. As we have seen it was not until 1833 that the Government felt that it was obliged to make any contribution to education at all, and when, in 1870, elementary education was introduced the responsibility for the provision of schools was given to decentralised schools boards throughout the country. The 1902 and 1918 Education Acts made no attempt to centralise control of education, though the 1902 Act reduced the number of local bodies. In 1944 the responsibility for the provision of education was given to 163 local education authorities, while as we have seen the President of the Board of Education was replaced by a Minister of Education. Twenty years later the Ministry of Education was expanded to include the Ministry for Science, and also to take responsibility for the universities, becoming the Department of Education and Science (DES), headed by a Secretary of State. The Secretary of State is responsible for framing and directing policy, and for the general supervision of the local education authorities, though he will not intervene at the local level unless it is felt that the authority is acting unreasonably.

It is often suggested that the Engish system of local authority control of education has advantages, as the system is more flexible than it would be if schools were directly under the control of a ministry. There is no central board of education to decide syllabus, teaching methods and other details, though the Department does lay down minimum standards and gives advice to the local authorities. Contact between the schools and the Secretary of State is maintained by officials known as Her Majesty's Inspectors of Schools (HMIs), who inspect schools and the teaching done in them, and also assist and advise individual teachers. Although as a general rule the syllabus and curriculum of a school are not laid down by statute, there is an exception. According to the 1944 Education Act, every school day must begin with a collective act of worship, and children must be given religious instruction (though parents can withdraw their children from both of these if they so wish).

While local control may have its advantages it can, as we have seen, produce problems. Local authorities are by no means of the same standard when it comes to providing educational facilities. Education can often become a political issue as party politics play an increasingly important part at local government level. This was certainly so in the case of comprehensive schools, particularly in the period between 1964 and 1970 when Conservative-controlled local education authorities tried to resist Labour plans to replace secondary modern schools and grammar schools.

Education committees consist of members of district councils in metropolitan counties and county councils elsewhere, together with co-opted experts (for example, the Professor of Education from the local university). The education committee is appointed by the council, which acts as the local education authority, and is responsible to it. The LEA also appoints a chief education officer, and it is this official who is responsible for administering education on a day-to-day basis in the LEA area. As we have seen, the LEA has the duty of providing primary, local and further education; some higher education, for example that provided by polytechnics, is an LEA responsibility, but universities are not. Education is financed from the rates (see p. 59) and also by a grant from the central government. It is the latter provision that ultimately gives the Secretary of State his power, should he choose to use it, for if the local authority refuses to accept his directions he can cut off funds.

SCHOOLS

Although local authorities are expected to provide nursery schools for children over the age of two, few are able to do this, in spite of the fact that there is considerable demand. For most authorities their responsibility begins when the child goes to the primary school at the age of five. Some primary schools are voluntary schools, originally built and maintained by the churches, but now largely dependent on the local authority for finance. In controlled schools the local authority is responsible for the maintenance of the school buildings, and appoints the majority of the school managers and members of the teaching staff. However the authority must consult the managers over the appointment of the head teacher and any teacher giving religious instruction. Most of the controlled schools are run by the Church of England. In the case of aided schools the managers are responsible for the fabric (i.e the buildings) of the school, though they can usually obtain financial assistance from the Department of Education and Science. Religious instruction in aided schools is controlled by the managers, two-thirds of whom are appointed by the religious body running the school.

Primary schools can be solely for juniors or have an infant section under the same roof. There are abut 23,000 primary schools with more than five million pupils in England and Wales. One of the great problems in many primary schools is the size of the classes, forty or more children to a class being only too common.

At the age of eleven children move from the primary school

to a secondary school; the kind of school this will be depends on whether the area in which the pupil lives has retained the old selective system or 'gone comprehensive'.

Grammar Schools

Grammar schools are of two main kinds: local authority grammar schools and 'direct grant' grammar schools, so called because they get a direct grant from the Department of Education. Direct grant schools are completely independent of the local authority, but in return for finance from the state they provide a number of places for children from the area administered by the LEA. The direct grant schools are often of considerable antiquity and most regard themselves as being superior to the schools under the control of the local authority. In December 1975 about 110 of the 173 direct grant grammar schools in England and Wales announced that they would go independent rather than co-operate in comprehensive schemes.

Many grammar schools, and particularly those in the larger towns, are single-sex schools, and very often one can find a boys' school and a girls' school (frequently called a 'high school') existing side by side. The grammar schools consider that their main purpose is to provide an academic education for their pupils and consequently there is considerable emphasis on examinations. The most important of these examinations is the General Certificate of Education (the GCE) which is in two parts. The first part is known as Ordinary or 'O' level, and this is taken at the age of fifteen or sixteen. Advanced level ('A' level) is usually taken after a further two years of study at eighteen. The GCE examinations are not set by a central body, but by boards appointed by the universities, for example the Northern Universities Joint Matriculation Board and the Oxford and Cambridge Schools Examination Board. Children who attend a grammar school are usually expected to sit at least the 'O' level GCE. The number of papers varies but few pupils will take more than ten, and most will take rather fewer. Many children leave school after sitting their 'O' levels and this means that it takes on the nature of a school-leaving examination. Others will, however, stay on at school and take the higher standard 'A' level papers, usually in three or four subjects. 'A' level is recognised as the initial qualification for most university and other higher education courses and also for some professions.

For most grammar schools success in the GCE examinations is a measure of the success of the school. Preparation for 'O' level starts quite early in the pupil's career, and if he is successful at the first stage he will be encouraged to stay on as a member of the Sixth Form (i.e. the two or three senior classes in the school) in order to study for 'A' levels.

As well as stressing the importance of examinations, the grammar school places great emphasis on out-of-school activities, particularly sports. If it is true, as has been suggested earlier, that many secondary modern schools imitate the grammar schools, it is also true that the grammar schools model themselves on the public schools. Most grammar schools, those for girls as well as those for boys, insist on school uniform, and the pupils are divided up into artificial 'houses', derived from the (residential) houses at public schools, for competitive purposes. In most schools senior pupils are given authority over the younger children, and are known as prefects or monitors. Some boys' schools have cadet forces where boys are given military and 'character' training.

Secondary Modern Schools

Originally secondary modern schools were conceived as schools for children who were less academic, though as we have seen they did not emulate the grammar schools. Many schools started preparing children for 'O' level courses, while in some cases Sixth Forms were established. In 1964 the Secretary of State tacitly recognised the change in the function of the secondary modern schools by instituting an examination designed specially for their pupils, the Certificate of Secondary Education (CSE).

Some secondary modern schools under the direction of an enthusiastic headmaster and teachers have developed special courses for their pupils, with encouraging results. In some schools pupils have managed to achieve good marks at 'O' level in spite of certain disadvantages, for example, larger classes and inferior equipment. A pupil from a secondary modern school who shows promise can transfer to a grammar school, though in practice this happens comparatively rarely. However a gifted child from a secondary modern background who has not had the chance to study for GCE can go to a college of further education and take the examinations there.

Whereas grammar schools tend to be single sex, secondary

modern schools are frequently co-educational. Secondary modern schools often have a poor staff/pupil ratio, particularly in industrial areas, as graduate teachers and those with higher qualifications usually tend to take jobs in grammar or public schools, where more advanced teaching is available.

Comprehensive Schools
We have already seen that during the second half of the sixties the provision of comprehensive schools became the subject of a major political controversy. Although the term comprehensive school is widely used it is not always appreciated that there are several different kinds of comprehensive school in England and Wales today. Circular 10/65 listed the following types:

1. The 'all-through' school, providing education from 11 to 18.
2. The 'two-tier' school, where children transfer from the primary school to a junior comprehensive at the age of 11, and then go to a senior comprehensive school at 13 or 14.
3. The parallel-tiered school, where only some children choose or are selected for the upper tier.
4. The tiered school, where children go from primary school to comprehensive at 11, and then at 13–14 have the option of going to either a senior school taking them past the school-leaving age, or one that provides education up to 15 (later 16).
5. Schools for ages 11–16, followed by sixth form colleges.
6. The three-tier system: primary schools 5 to 8–9, comprehensive school 8–9 to 12–13, comprehensive senior school 12 to 13-plus.

The type of school most favoured by the circular was the 11–18 school.

Opposition to comprehensive schools came from many quarters – parents, politicians, teachers, educationalists and others. One of the main reasons for their attitude was that comprehensivation implied the end of the grammar schools, though it is interesting to note that few defended the secondary modern schools, beyond saying that they knew of 'some very good secondary modern schools'. Undoubtedly much of the opposition was on political grounds. Many Conservative councillors and Members of Parliament are on record as having said that they favoured the creation of an intellectual elite, such as that provided by the grammar schools. Many teachers and educationalists who opposed the introduction of comprehensive schools did so, not because they favoured an elite, but because they were opposed to the way comprehensive schools were being established. The popular view of a comprehensive school is a large purpose-built campus providing a complete range of educational facilities, staffed with sufficient specialists to ensure that the children get the widest possible education, provided in small teaching groups. It is unlikely that even the most impassioned supporter of comprehensive schools could argue that this is always the reality. In many cases the schools, formed by the amalgamation of existing grammar and secondary modern schools, have carried on in the old buildings. Many of these date from the beginning of the century, or even earlier, and often the buildings are separated from each other by busy streets, while in some country areas they are even in different towns.

The basic idea of the comprehensive school is to provide an education for children of all ranges of ability. In most grammar and secondary modern schools classes are 'streamed' in terms of the all-round ability of the child. The disadvantage of this system is that children who are good at one or two subjects may be placed in a low stream because of weakness in other subjects. The comprehensive schools try, as far as possible, to take account of this by dividing children into groups, according to their ability in different subjects. To do this efficiently obviously requires a large staff and a large number of pupils, with the result that comprehensive schools are often accused of being large impersonal institutions, where the children have difficulty in getting to know one another, let alone members of the teaching staff.

Independent Schools
To many people English education means the public schools, which conjure up an image of boys in striped blazers and straw boaters playing exotic games, and being educated in buildings that are more reminiscent of medieval castles or Victorian railway stations than educational establishments. In fact in terms of numbers the public schools comprise a very small minority of the schools in England. Only 5 per cent of the school population receive their education in such institutions. In terms of influence, and prestige, however, their importance is very great.

There is no exact definition of a public school, though one thing a public school is *not* is public in the usual sense of the word. Originally 'public' meant that a school was run by a governing body 'in the public interest', as opposed to private schools that were run for the benefit of their proprietor. Today the public schools are usually held to be the two hundred or so schools whose headmasters belong to the Headmasters' Conference (the HMC), though recently the heads of some state schools have been invited to join this body. Traditionally a school whose headmaster belongs to the HMC must have a certain degree of independence from the state, a Sixth Form above a certain size, and a good proportion of pupils entering universities each year. Apart from the recently admitted state schools, the HMC schools include about 140 schools that are financed independently and some 64 direct grant grammar schools.

Public schools draw their finances from fees (which can be well over £1,000 a year), from trusts and endowments, and from land and property. In recent years a useful source of extra money has been that provided by industry for the building of science laboratories or teaching rooms. Whereas direct grant grammar schools receive money from the state, and in return reserve a proportion of their places for scholarship boys, public schools receive no state support and have few scholarship places.

Some public schools are very ancient: Winchester was founded in 1394 and Eton in 1440. But the majority of the schools were established during the nineteenth century to provide secondary education for middle- and upper-class boys, who would go on to the universities of Oxford or Cambridge and thence into the professions or the Church (of England).

Although the number of public schools is very small in comparison with other secondary schools, they have a great influence on society in Britain as a whole. If one looks at the educational background of politicians of all parties, of civil servants, High Court judges, leading Churchmen, prominent industrialists and high-ranking officers in the armed forces, one finds an overwhelming number of public school educated men. The power of the 'old school tie' can play a considerable part in getting a university place, particularly at Oxford and Cambridge, or a certain kind of job. This is not to say that having been to public school guarantees a university place, or a good job, but it does tend to make life easier.

Most public schools are boarding schools and the majority of them are single-sex institutions, catering for boys. There are a number of public-school-type establishments for girls, most of them of recent foundation, and a few co-educational boarding schools, though usually these are rather far removed from the conventional public school idea. Parents wishing their son to enter a public school may have to put his name down for the school a number of years before he is old enough to go there. Children destined for public schools frequently attend private preparatory (or prep) schools between the ages of five and thirteen, after which they transfer to the public school. Although a child intending to go to a public school does not have to take the 11-plus, he does have to sit for the 'Common Entrance' examination. If he passes this examination he goes to the school of his or rather his parents' choice. In practice few boys whose parents have the means to send them to a public school fail to gain a place, though this may not always be at the school of their first choice. Factors such as family connections with the school also play a not unimportant part in selection. Not all those intending to go to a public school attend a prep school; some go through the state primary system and then on to a public school, though there are problems here, one being the difference in the age at which transfer is made. In some cases children who fail the 11-plus, and whose parents can afford to pay for their education, continue their education in the private sector.

It may seem strange that parents are prepared to pay large school fees every year when it is possible to get free education at the state's expense. Some parents, however, consider that the advantages of the independent schools is such that the money they pay in fees is a worthwhile investment. Not only do boys from public schools enjoy a certain prestige later in life, but the public schools are often able, by offering status and fringe benefits, to attract higher qualified staff. Classes in public schools are usually smaller than those in state schools so that pupils receive more individual attention.

The exclusive nature of the public schools has received much criticism in recent years. A number of committees have been set up to consider ways in which the independent schools could be incorporated into the state system but their recommendations have not been acted upon. In 1944 the Fleming Committee suggested that public schools should offer at least 25 per cent of their places to pupils from state primary schools. The Newsom Committee, set up in 1965 by the Labour Government to consider how the public schools could be best integrated with the state system, recommended that up to 50 per cent of the places at boarding schools should be made generally available. After the defeat of Labour in 1970 the Newsom Committee was disbanded and its proposals shelved. It seems unlikely that the public schools will ever be closed by parliamentary legislation, as such a measure would almost certainly arouse a great deal of opposition from the schools and their influential supporters. On the other hand if state schools can improve their standards, in terms of size of classes and the provision of facilities, it is possible that the numbers of parents willing to spend a large sum of money on a private education will decrease.

In addition to the public schools there are a number of other independent schools, some of which are run as businesses by their proprietors (many preparatory schools are of this type). Others are run along experimental or 'progressive' lines, the best known probably being Summerhill, founded by A. S. Neill.

Independent schools are open to inspection by the Department of Education and Science and must be 'recognised as efficient'. Schools not meeting the Department's requirements may be required to close though they have the right of appeal against closure to an independent tribunal.

Scotland

In Scotland overall responsibility for schools rests with the Secretary of State for Scotland, though at the local level there are education committees not unlike those found south of the border. Primary schools are usually administered and supported by the education authorities. The majority of Scottish children of secondary school age are educated in comprehensive schools. The secondary school certificate examination is known as the Scottish Certificate of Education. Scotland also has some grant-aided and independent schools (the term 'public school' in Scotland refers to state primary schools).

HIGHER EDUCATION

Broadly speaking, 'higher education' covers universities, polytechnics and colleges of education. There are forty-five universities in Britain, some of which, as collegiate institutions, have a number of different parts. London, for example, has more than twenty colleges and several medical schools attached to hospitals, while the University of Wales consists of six separate, but linked, institutions. There are also thirty-one polytechnics and over 100 colleges of education. During the academic year 1973–4 there were 224,000 students in the universities, 208,000 in polytechnics and 110,700 in the colleges of education; by 1981 the figures are expected to be 375,000, 335,000 and 80,000 respectively. At the beginning of the sixties there were about 100,000 students at the universities and about the same number at other higher education institutions. Worried that Britain was not providing sufficient places in higher education (in 1957 only 7 per cent of the 17/18 age group were entering full-time higher education, in 1960 8.2 per cent), the government in 1961 appointed the Robbins Committee to report on higher education needs. When the Committee reported in 1964 it recommended that sufficient places should be available for all those requiring them. The report of the Committee was supplemented by a large number of tables showing the expansion that was expected to take place in the immediate future. In fact expansion was much more rapid than predicted, particularly in non-university institutions. In 1967–8 there were 200,000 students at universities (Robbins had predicted 197,000), 106,000 at colleges of education (Robbins: 84,000), and 71,000 at other institutions of higher education (Robbins: 47,000). This meant that there were 376,000 students in higher education, 14.3 per cent of the 17–18 age group and 52,000 more than Robbins had expected. Robbins had forecast that between the academic year 1962–3 and that of 1967–8 there would be a growth rate of 51 per cent; in fact the growth rate was 74 per cent. The increase in the number of students during the sixties meant that many of the universities expanded considerably, while a number of new ones were created, as will be explained in the next section. In addition a number of polytechnics were established, usually based on institutions that already existed (see p. 110).

Universities

At the beginning of the nineteenth century there were seven universities in Britain, only two of which were in England. By the beginning of the twentieth century a further five had been founded, while between 1900 and the mid-sixties another thirty-four universities were granted charters, which means that at the present time Britain has forty-five universities. (Although thirty-four universities were established between 1900 and 1970, one was lost – Trinity College, Dublin – when Ireland became independent in 1922.)

The oldest universities in Britain are Oxford and Cambridge – often referred to jointly as 'Oxbridge '– founded at the end of the twelfth century. Until the reign of Henry II it had been the custom for English scholars to study at universities on the continent, particularly at the University of Paris. Henry's quarrel with his archbishop, Thomas à Becket, led to the expulsion of Englishmen studying in France and the refugees set up their own institution at Oxford. Later some members of the Oxford community moved to Cambridge. The first Oxford college, University College, was founded in about 1249; the first Cambridge one, Peterhouse, in 1284. No further universities were established in England until the nineteenth century, though four were founded in Scotland between 1411 and 1582, while in 1591 Queen Elizabeth I granted a charter to Trinity College, Dublin.

Both Oxford and Cambridge restricted their membership to members of the Anglican Church until the nineteenth century, with the result that at various times the Dissenters (Nonconformists) tried to set up their own higher education institutions. Although some of these had considerable success in the short term, they were unable to establish themselves as universities. It was not until the 1830s when the universities of Durham and London opened their doors that non-Anglicans were admitted to higher education.

During the second half of the nineteenth century a number of institutes for advanced education were set up, particularly in the north of England. Some of these, such as Owen's College in Manchester and the Yorkshire College at Leeds, were to develop into universities in their own right at the turn of the century. These universities, which include Manchester, Liverpool and Bristol, are often referred to as 'the civic universities', though they are more popularly known as 'red-brick universities', a name said to be derived from the colour of the building material of the University of Birmingham.

The second-generation civic universities, include a number of institutions that started life as university colleges, that is university-level institutions which could not award their own degrees. Instead they prepared students for the 'external degrees' of the University of London. These institutions acquired full university status just before, or shortly after, the Second World War. Universities of this kind include Leicester, Hull and Nottingham.

In 1949 the University College of North Staffordshire (later the University of Keele) was founded. Although a university college, this institution awarded its own degrees from the start, as has been the case with all universities founded since 1949. The universities of the sixties fall into two categories: in the first place there were the 'new' universities, completely new foundations, usually situated on the outskirts of provincial towns like Brighton (the University of Sussex) and York. Secondly there were the former colleges of advanced technology, which formed the basis of technological universities, for example Loughborough, Bradford and Salford. Seven of the 'new' universities were set up in England, one in Scotland, and one in Ulster. England was also given seven technological universities, while two more were established in Scotland.

The last university that should be mentioned is the Open University (see p. 109), which accepted its first students in 1970.

British universities therefore have been founded at different times, in response to different needs. Thus there is little apparent similarity between the University of Oxford, founded in the thirteenth century mainly for the training of priests, and the University of Loughborough, founded in the 1960s, which is primarily concerned with producing technologists and engineers. Another reason for differences is that universities have always been planned and set up at the local level, even when the greater part of their funds have come from the state. Thus, even when a number of universities have been founded at the same time, their structures may differ considerably. For example, York, Kent, Sussex and Norwich were all established during the sixties. The first two have a collegiate system, derived from the ancient universities; the other two have a structure that is more like that of the civic universities, though with many distinctive features. The type and content of courses may also differ a great deal from university to university, as may entrance requirements, staff-student ratios, teaching methods and so on.

Nevertheless in spite of the differences between the social and academic environments of the universities there are certain features that they all have in common. In the first place there are no state universities in Britain. Although the state provides over 70 per cent of the money required by the universities – and about 90 per cent towards capital programmes – it has no direct control over how the money is spent. Of course if the government felt that grants were being used for unsuitable purposes it could cut off funds. There is little doubt, however, that such an action would produce an outcry that academic freedom was in danger, and so it seems clear that a government would interfere only in a very extreme case. Grants to the universities are distributed through the University Grants Committee (UGC), which is made up of representatives of the academic and business communities. The UGC also advises the Secretary of State, and the Minister of State responsible for higher education, on university affairs.

Secondly the standards for first degrees are intended to be the same at all universities, though in practice one university may have greater prestige than another. In England and Wales, studying for a first degree normally takes three years, except for subjects such as medicine and dentistry where courses are invariably longer. At the end of a first degree course the successful student is awarded a Bachelor's degree, usually a Bachelor of Arts (BA) or Bachelor of Science (BSc). In Scotland the first degree is a Master's degree which is awarded after four years of study. In English and Welsh universities a Master's degree is awarded after a further period of study, except at Oxford and Cambridge where it is possible to purchase an MA twelve years after graduating as a BA. The names and standards of higher degrees vary between different universities.

As far as the administration of universities is concerned there is a basic similarity between the various institutions, though details may differ. In England and Wales the nominal head of the university is the Chancellor, who is usually a distinguished public figure, often a member of the royal family or the aristocracy. The Chancellor appears at degree-giving ceremonies and on other appropriate occasions, but his duties are almost completely ceremonial and he takes no part in the day-to-day running of the university. The professional head of the university is the Vice-Chancellor, who in most cases is an academic of professorial rank. At most universities the Vice-Chancellorship is a permament position, but at Oxford the office is held by heads of colleges for a period of three years.

The bodies and committees which run the administrative and academic side of the university vary from institution to institution. In some universities members of the academic staff and students have far more say than in others, while obviously the vast collegiate University of London, with over 22,000 students and 800 professors in more than thirty schools, requires a totally different structure from that of a small provincial institution such as Keele, with some 1,900 students and fewer than thirty professors. Nevertheless there are certain features that are common to most universities and these are outlined below.

The University Court is usually a large body consisting of local dignitaries, such as Members of Parliament, local councillors, church leaders and others, together with members of the academic staff. However in most cases the powers of the Court are purely formal. Executive control of the university is vested in the Council, composed of persons nominated by the Court, local authorities and senior academics. The Council is principally concerned with finance and seeing that the university is able to meet its responsibilities.

The Senate is the principal academic body of the university. It is responsible for academic policy, teaching, examinations and discipline. The Senate is usually made up mainly of senior academics, though there is a trend towards including more junior members of staff and in some cases students, too. Academic work is the responsibility of faculties, each of which is headed by a Dean. A faculty consists of a number of departments, and the head of department is usually a professor. Large departments will often have more than one professor, and may be subdivided according to the particular interests of the holders of the professorial chairs. The position of 'reader' is usually reserved for senior members of staff with strong research interests, and in some cases a reader may in fact be the head of a small department. Senior lecturers and lecturers are responsible for much of the teaching provided by the department, but they are also expected to engage in research.

Most academic staff divide their time between teaching and research, and in the case of senior staff they may often find that they have a considerable administrative load as well. Most university teaching, at least in the arts and social sciences, is done through lectures, supplemented by tutorials and seminars. The amount of individual attention given to students varies from one university to another. At Oxbridge great emphasis is put on the tutorial system, and students receive a considerable amount of personal tuition. At many provincial universities, however, the weekly tutorial, where students are taught in small groups, is not possible. The British universities have, with some justification, prided themselves on their favourable staff-student ratio. At the beginning of the seventies there was a member of staff to every 8.1 students. However it seems likely that by the end of the decade the figure will be nearer 1:10.

During the late sixties and into the seventies staff-student relations came under a certain amount of strain at some universities. Many students considered that university administrators (and to a lesser extent lecturers) were not really concerned about students and their problems. In a number of cases they took militant action in order to bring their grievances to the notice of the authorities (a common cause of discontent was the lack of student representation in the university administration). In some universities little attention was paid to the students' case, a reaction which usually inflamed the situation still further, but at others the protestors gained a sympathetic hearing, and in many cases reforms followed or were promised.

The Open University The Open University was granted its charter in 1969, and started to enrol its first students the following year. Originally the Open University was conceived as 'the university of the second chance', designed to provide degree-level courses for those who for one reason or another had been unable to take advantage of a conventional university education when they left school. There are no formal entrance requirements and recent advertisements for the university have emphasised that people from all occupations are eligible to become students. In spite of hopes that the university would achieve a significant break through in providing university education for people who were excluded from the conventional system, a large proportion of the first students were teachers seeking to improve their qualifications. Some people have gone as far as to say that the Open University is a failure because it has not reached the people for whom it was intended. On the other hand, the Open University on the eve of its first graduation day had nearly 40,000 students, which indicates that it is filling a a need. In 1974 the University took its first 500 school-leavers.

There are no conventional lectures or classes. Students study in their own homes with the aid of lectures broadcast on television and radio supplemented by course material prepared by tutors. The Open University has thirteen regional directors, each responsible for providing support services for the students in his area. The regional director maintains contact with local organisations, such as libraries, and local education authorities, and with the headquarters of the Open University at Milton Keynes. He also runs local study centres and appoints local counsellors and course tutors. Counsellors are expected to help students with any educational problems they may encounter, while tutors hold courses for students in local study centres. Students are also expected to attend a summer school each year.

For the authorities one of the attractions of the Open University is that it is relatively cheap. It is estimated that the average recurrent cost per student at the Open University is a quarter of that for a conventional university, and as more students are enrolled so costs per student fall.

Polytechnics

The Robbins Committee recommended that 'higher education' should be concentrated in the universities, while 'further education', non-degree level courses, should be given in local authority colleges and technical institutions. However in 1966 the Labour Government announced that it intended to develop higher education outside the university sector, and designate a number of polytechnics. These polytechnics gradually came into being during the late sixties and early seventies. In most cases polytechnics were formed from institutions that already existed (for example in some cities the college of technology, the college of commerce and the college of art were combined); in others, an entirely new institution was set up. The amalgamations meant that many newly designated polytechnics found that they were expected to continue to operate in the buildings occupied by the constituent parts. In some areas polytechnics did get new buildings, though it is significant that these were for the most part much less lavish than those occupied by the new universities.

Polytechnics are financed and controlled by local authorities.

The number of students taking degree courses differs from institution to institution; at some 90 per cent or more of the students are reading for degrees, but elsewhere the figure is much lower. Some of the institutions designated as polytechnics have had degree-level courses for many years, but nearly all of these were the somewhat rigid London University external degrees. In 1964 the Council for National Academic Awards (CNAA) was established, and today a large number of polytechnic students are working for CNAA degrees. Under the CNAA scheme polytechnics draw up their own courses which are then submitted to the appropriate Council board for approval. In order for a course to be accepted the polytechnic must convince the board that the standard of lecturers teaching the course and the facilities that the polytechnic can offer, in terms of library size or laboratories, are satisfactory.

The events of the sixties seem to have produced a certain amount of rivalry between universities and polytechnics. Some university staff seem to regard polytechnics as 'jumped-up colleges', while lecturers in polytechnics in their turn feel that many of the universities are out of touch with the real developments that are taking place in higher education. One point that often causes bitterness is that polytechnics are subject to local authority control, while at universities there is a great deal of freedom from outside interference.

Colleges of Education

Colleges of Education, designed for training teachers, are going through a difficult time at the moment; some have been closed and the future or others is under review. A recent circular from the Department of Education and Science suggested that the ideal college of education in the future should be between 1,000 and 2,000 students. Those that have fewer than this number, a large proportion at the present time, should join the local polytechnic, and in fact a number of these link-ups have been confirmed. An increasing number of college of education students are taking degree level courses, many of them leading to the degree of Bachelor of Education (B.Ed).

Students

Students taking full-time degree courses at universities, colleges of education and polytechnics are entitled to study grants from their local education authority. At the beginning of the 1975-6 academic year the basic grant stood at £740. Parents with an income of more than £2,200 a year are expected to contribute to their child's upkeep, the parental contribution being assessed according to a sliding scale. Many students criticise the grants system because it takes parental income into account. They say that they should be treated as independent individuals rather than as children dependent on their parents. Another source of discontent is the existence of the means test, whereby parental income is assessed. In the last few years students have been trying to bring pressure on the authorities to raise the level of student grants. One result of this is that some people have suggested that students should be given loans, which would be paid back after the students have finished their courses, but the suggestion has not been accepted either by students or the Department of Education and Science.

Students at British universities tend to be younger than those at many similar institutions on the continent. One reason for this is probably the fact since the majority of courses only last for three years, and this is the period for which the grant is paid, students spend a relatively short time on their studies. The majority of British students go to university straight from school at the age of eighteen, which means that they have completed their studies by the time they are twenty-one or twenty-two. As there is no military service, boys as well as girls are able to continue their studies from sixth form to higher education without a break. Many of the students at polytechnics are older than those at universities, as they may well have served in industry or commerce for some years before coming to take a degree. Indeed many courses at polytechnics are 'sandwich courses', where engineers or trainee managers will work for a qualification at the same time as doing a job. A relatively small number of students are married. This is partly due to the fact that most students are quite young and also because, until recently, if two students married the wife's grant was greatly reduced. Many students therefore preferred to live together without getting married, and receive two full grants, rather than exist in 'respectable' poverty on a much smaller amount. In 1975 the regulations were changed, though not as radically as the NUS (National Union of Students) had hoped.

Facilities for students vary greatly between universities. The standard of accommodation at some Oxbridge colleges is very high indeed; students have well-appointed rooms and servants provided by the college. At the other end of the scale, students are expected to compete for flats and bed-sitters on the open market. Most of the new universities try to provide student hostels or halls of residence, and a number of the older institutions have also been building these whenever possible. In general the amenities enjoyed by university students are superior to those for polytechnic students.

Students wishing to attend a university in England must first apply to the Central Council on University Admissions, giving details of their qualifications, or expected qualifications, and the course they wish to follow. They also list the universities of their choice in order of preference. The Council then forwards the applications to the universities who make the decision whether to accept or reject the candidate. Students wishing to study at a polytechnic apply directly.

FURTHER EDUCATION

Further education is provided by colleges of further education and technical colleges, which are financed and administered by local authorities. These colleges provide a wide range of technical and vocational training, to full-time or part-time students. Many full-time students are studying for GCE examinations, perhaps with the intention of going on to take a degree, though others are taking courses that will qualify them for a particular career. A large number of the students at technical colleges are taking day-release courses – in other words they are working in a factory or workshop for four days a week and attending the college on the other day – or block release courses, which means that they attend full-time for a period of two months or so.

There are a wide range of adult education and 'extra-mural' classes available throughout the country, run by extra mural departments of the universities, the Workers' Educational Association and local education authorities. Subjects covered include languages, local history, archaeology, painting, judo, cookery, pottery, photography and a host of others.

7

The Industrial State

During the Middle Ages England, like the rest of Europe, was a rural country. Most of the population lived in villages or small country settlements and depended on agriculture for the necessities of life. The sixteenth and seventeenth centuries brought important developments in political and economic life, but as technological advances did not keep pace with these the pattern of life did not change a great deal. It was not until the beginning of the eighteenth century that technological developments began to catch up with changes in the political and economic system; once they did, however, the effect was dramatic. Inventions such as those by Newcomen, Watt, Darby and Kay were to change Britain, in a relatively short period of time, from a rural nation dependent on agriculture to an urban one growing rich on the power of the machine.

Towards the end of the seventeenth century a number of financial institutions began to develop in Britain, the most important being the Bank of England, founded in 1694. The existence of a comparatively sophisticated financial structure through which credit could be obtained did a great deal to encourage the development of trade and industry during the next century. Other important factors included a plentiful supply of raw materials in Britain, such as coal and iron ore, and Britain's trading position astride the sea routes to the New World.

By the early years of the nineteenth century Britain had won a commanding lead over the rest of the world as far as industrialisation was concerned and proceeded to exploit its position. Its dominance of world trade was to be of relatively short duration and by the end of the 1870s it was virtually over. Nevertheless, in spite of increasing competition Britain managed to retain her lead in a number of fields, while the City of London continued to be the centre of world trade well into the twentieth century.

At the end of the nineteenth century Britain's main rivals in the struggle for economic leadership were Germany, united under the leadership of Bismarck after the Franco-Prussian War, and the United States, which was fast developing its industrial potential. Before the end of the century both these countries had overtaken the United Kingdom in the production of steel. By 1900 the USA was making twice as much steel as the UK (USA 10.1 million tons, Germany 6.2 million tons, UK 4.9 million tons). The First World War and the economic difficulties of the inter-war years caused many problems for Britain, though in 1938 it still accounted for about 22 per cent of the world's exports of manufactured goods. This figure has been declining since the Second World War as international competition has grown more intense, and at the beginning of the 1970s stood at 11 per cent.

One of Britain's major problems in the post-war period is that its balance of payments position has been far from satisfactory. For many years, even though its position as an exporter of manufactured goods declined, Britain was able to sustain itself on 'invisible exports' such as the financial services provided by the City of London, tourism, and shipping and aviation services. However in recent years the value of these invisible exports has not been sufficient to cover the trade deficit.

Since the Second World War successive governments have tried to come to grips with Britain's economic difficulties using a variety of measures. The pound was devalued in 1949 and again in 1967 and since June 1972 it has been allowed to float, which produced an effective devaluation against the dollar of 30 per cent by the beginning of December 1975. Britain's problems during the seventies have been accentuated by the general world recession and the sharp increases in commodity and oil prices. The result has been a stagnation in domestic growth, inflation running at an unprecedented level and unemployment over the million mark (during the summer of 1975). (See also pp. 142-4.)

Nevertheless Britain remains an important industrial nation and manufactured goods comprise over 80 per cent of its exports. Engineering products including industrial machinery, motor vehicles, electrical equipment, aerospace products, ships and agricultural machinery are the largest single group of exports, but chemicals, metals, textiles and food and drink are also important. Britain's most important trading partners are the countries of Western Europe, the United States, and Commonwealth and former Commonwealth countries such as Canada, Australia, South Africa and Ireland.

In spite of present economic difficulties, there are signs that circumstances may improve. Britain is now a member of the EEC with all the trading benefits that this confers and there are hopes that before long North Sea oil will make Britain far less dependent on imported oil. The Government has also announced plans to encourage investment in industry.

THE BRITISH ECONOMY TODAY

During the nineteenth century the policy of both Liberal and Conservative Governments was to interfere as little as possible in the commercial life of the country. The general belief was that trade was best left in the hands of the businessman. This *laissez-faire* attitude might have been acceptable when Britain dominated world trade, but increasing competition in international markets, to say nothing of the complexity of managing the domestic economy, have meant that twentieth-century governments have had to take a much greater part in economic planning. Government participation in economic decision-making has increased to such an extent that during the fifties a Conservative minister could say, 'We are all planners now.' It is particularly significant that a Conservative should say this, because the Conservative Party holds the view that the economy should operate with the minimum of government intervention. The Labour Party on the other hand believes that the economy should be managed for the benefit of society as a whole, and this, they claim, is only possible if key industries are under the control of the state. During periods when the Labour Party has been in office a certain amount of nationalisation has taken place, but the great majority of manufacturing companies are still run by private enterprise. At present Britain has a mixed economy; the iron and steel industry, coal-mining, the railways and some other areas of transport, public utilities such as gas and electricity and a number of other industries are controlled by the state. In addition the Government has substantial holdings in a number of companies, for example British Petroleum and British Leyland.

As in other countries, the last few decades have given rise to a large number of amalgamations between companies, the result of take-overs or mergers. As a result certain sectors of industry are dominated by a small number of large companies. The production of motor vehicles, for example, is concentrated almost completely in the hands of four companies, three of which are controlled by large American concerns. Mergers in the aerospace industry have produced two large corporations which between them account for virtually all the aircraft built in Britain. The aerospace and ship-building industries are also being taken under state control.

Control of Industry

State Ownership Up until 1945 nationalisation had been on a relatively small scale, but the Labour Government that came to power in that year was committed to a comprehensive nation-alisation programme. In 1946 the Bank of England was taken over by the state, to be followed in the same year by the coal-mines and civil aviation. The Transport Act of 1947 nationalised the railways, canals and some road transport, while in 1948 and 1949 gas and iron and steel were added to the list (electricity had been nationalised in 1926). The Conservatives denationalised iron and steel in 1953, but the industry was taken over again by the Labour Government in 1967. The Labour Party does not have a monopoly of nationalisation, however, for in 1954 the Conservatives set up the United Kingdom Atomic Energy Authority to develop nuclear power for peaceful purposes. In 1971 another Conservative Government nationalised Rolls-Royce after financial difficulties drove the company into liquida-tion.

It can scarcely be said that the nationalised industries have had an easy history. The establishment of the public sector and its role has produced a great deal of discussion in Parliament, in board rooms throughout the country and in a large number of other places. One of the issues that has caused most argument is how the public industries should be run. The fundamental question here is whether they should be expected to make a profit or whether they should be operated primarily as a public service, being subsidised when necessary by the government. This problem is well illustrated by the railways. When the railways were nationalised by the Transport Act of 1947 they had been making a loss for a number of years. Public ownership did not change the situation, and the question of profit versus public service was soon being hotly debated. The Act nationalising the railways had said that they should pay their way but a large labour force (648,740 workers in 1948), outdated equipment and a large number of uneconomic branch lines made this difficult to achieve. In 1963, however, the then chairman of British Railways, Dr Richard Beeching, published his rationalisation plan, which recommended that track mileage should be cut from 17,000 to 8,000, and that 70,000 jobs should be phased out. The report produced an immediate outcry from the public, who stood to lose their rail services, and from the railway unions, whose members were threatened with redundancy. A long and bitter discussion ensued as to whether Beeching's proposals should be implemented. On commercial grounds his findings made a great deal of sense. The railways had been planned for the needs of the nineteenth century, before road transport had developed on any scale. Fierce competition between rival companies meant that in some cases main lines duplicated each other, while country lines had lost much of their traffic to other forms of transport, particularly the family car. Nevertheless there were large numbers of people who did not have cars and for whom withdrawal of services would cause hardship, and it was for this reason that Beeching's critics argued that social costs should also be taken into consideration when planning future rail services, as the railways were owned by the state. Taking social costs into account would, of course, mean that financial subsidies would have to be provided. In the event, many of Beeching's proposals were adopted; but British Rail continued to lose money.

Similar problems have arisen in the case of other nationalised industries. In November 1974 it was announced that in future nationalised industries would be expected to pay their way.

Nationalised industries are controlled by government-appointed boards. It is these boards, under a chairman, who is also a government appointee, which are responsible for the day-to-day management of the particular industry. Overall control is in the hands of the appropriate minister, for example the Minister for Transport Industries within the Department of the Environment is responsible for the railways. Acting on behalf of the government, the minister appoints board members and can also dismiss them. He also has financial powers and, in consultation with the chairman and the board, decides matters of policy. Each year the board of each nationalised industry submits a report to Parliament, and this can be the subject of a debate or of Parliamentary Questions. Since 1957 a House of Commons Select Committee on the Nationalised Industries has examined the reports and accounts of the industries and reported back its findings to the House. Neither the boards of state-controlled concerns, nor their staff, are civil servants. Thus when the Post Office became a public corporation in 1969 – it had previously been a government department under the Postmaster-General – its employees lost their status as civil servants, becoming employees of a nationalised industry like the coalminers and the railwaymen.

In 1975 the Industry Bill was introduced. One of the objectives of the Bill was the establishment of a National Enterprise Board, with borrowing powers of £1,000 million. The objective of the Board was 'to establish, develop or maintain' industrial enterprises. The Bill was opposed by the Conservatives who felt that it would lead to further nationalisation.

Private Enterprise While control of the industries in the public sector is ultimately in the hands of Parliament, in the private sector control is vested in those who have a financial interest in a particular company. In most private companies ownership is concentrated in a few hands, and in practice the directors of a large number of small businesses are members of the same family. Expansion inevitably requires capital and in the first instance this often means a loan from a bank or similar institution. Really large-scale developments, however, are frequently financed by 'going public', which means that members of the public are given a chance to invest money in the company and thus participate in its fortunes. Money is invested by buying stocks or shares on the London Stock Exchange or one of the provincial exchanges. Stocks are loans, either to the government (gilt-edged) or to companies, which earn a fixed-interest return. Shares, however, mean that the purchaser actually becomes an owner of the company in which he is investing his money, though this ownership may well be shared with several thousand other people. The shareholders as owners of the company are responsible for appointing the board of directors, who run the company on their behalf. In practice the majority of shareholders are more interested in receiving their dividend than in interfering with how the company is run, and so most boards of directors tend to be self-perpetuating.

As mentioned earlier, recent years have seen a trend towards amalgamations between companies. For some years after the Second World War the pattern was one of large companies buying up their smaller competitors. Although this process still continues the emphasis during the sixties switched towards mergers between groups of comparable size. Thus in 1967 the National Provincial Bank combined with the Westminster Bank, becoming the National Westminster Bank, and in 1968 British Motor Holdings and Leyland merged to form the British Leyland Motor Corporation, while a similar pattern was seen in industries as diverse as electronics and food and also in retail trade. These amalgamations were so far-reaching in their scope that it has been estimated that by the end of 1968 40 per cent of the total assets of all firms in the manufacturing industry were held by twenty-eight giant companies. The scale of the mergers and the concentration of economic power in fewer hands disturbed the government of the day, and in 1965 the powers of the Board of Trade (now part of the enlarged Department of Trade and Industry) to investigate mergers were increased. In 1965 the Monopolies and Mergers Act strengthened the Monopolies Commission that had originally been established in 1948. If the Commission considers that a merger is not in the public interest it can recommend government intervention. Another body that is designed to ensure fair trading is the Restrictive Practices Court, set up in 1956 to investigate agreements on trading and prices made between business enterprises. If the Court feels that it is against the public interest for businesses to agree prices among themselves it can declare that the arrangement is illegal. In some cases, for example in publishing, the Court has found that resale price maintenance (RPM) works for the benefit of the public.

The government also intervenes in other aspects of economic life. In 1962 the National Economic Development Council, popularly known as Neddy, was formed. The Council consists of representatives of government, management and trade unions and meets at regular intervals under the chairmanship of the Prime Minister to discuss the future development of the economy. Each of the principal manufacturing industries has its own economic development committee (EDC) as do certain service and distribution industries. Like the NEDC, EDCs have members from government ministries, management and the trade unions. It is the role of each EDC to review the position of the industry for which it is responsible, and to take steps to make it more efficient.

The City

The City is roughly a square mile of banking houses, insurance firms and stockbrokers' offices, rubbing shoulders with such famous buildings as St Paul's Cathedral and the Tower of London. Although no longer the axis around which world trade revolves, London is still a financial centre of considerable importance. It is the largest international insurance market in the world, has important markets for the supply of goods and services, such as the Baltic Exchange and the London Metal Exchange, and is also the centre of the Sterling Area.

The financial power of the City originated centuries ago. During the Middle Ages merchants from London pioneered the wool trade with the continent. In Tudor times the City invested in the voyages of explorers and privateers such as Sir Francis Drake, while the support of the City for the parliamentary cause was one of the reasons for the defeat of Charles I in the Civil War. Many of the great institutions of the City were first established during the seventeenth century. In the 1680s Edward Lloyd's coffee house, from which grew the great insurance firm of Lloyd's, began its operations, while in the last decade of the century the Bank of England was founded.

The Bank of England The Bank of England was founded in 1694. It is interesting to note that, although it became banker to the government and the leading bank of issue, it was not until 1946 that the Bank was nationalised. It is no doubt due to this long period of independence that the Bank still operates with a certain amount of autonomy. Indeed at times some MPs, particularly Labour MPs, have complained that the Bank has too much freedom of action and should be controlled more closely.

The Bank of England plays a very important role in the commercial life of the United Kingdom. In addition to acting as banker to the government, it is also banker for overseas central banks and commercial banks in Britain. In England and Wales all bank notes are issued by the Bank of England, though in Scotland and Northern Ireland a number of banks have this right. The Bank is also the manager of the Exchange Equalisation Account, which consists of gold and foreign currency. By use of this the Bank can give support to the pound sterling in adverse market conditions. If, for example, there is large-scale conversion of pounds into German marks, the Bank can supply marks from the account and take sterling in exchange.

In addition to the responsibilities outlined above, the Bank also acts as a middle-man between the commercial institutions of the City and the government. It advises the government on monetary matters, and is also expected to ensure that the measures adopted by the government are put into effect. Methods employed by the Bank for implementing government policy include the regulation of interest rates and the buying and selling of Treasury bills. The head of the Bank is the Governor, a government appointee, and he presides over a board of directors, also chosen by the government.

Other Banks The most important clearing banks are the 'Big Four', Midland, Barclays, National Westminster and Lloyds, branches or associates of which can be found in virtually every High Street in Britain. The clearing banks between them provide the bulk of the banking services required by the British people: current and deposit accounts, short term loans and advice on financial matters. The banks are closely involved in many aspects of national and international finance and some of the banking groups also have extensive overseas interests.

Other Financial Institutions The merchant banks play an important role in London's activities as a commercial centre. Although there are some sixty concerns which could be described as merchant banks, the most exclusive are the seventeen which belong to the Accepting Houses Committee. The merchant banks are involved in a wide range of activities. Some specialise while others are active in a number of different fields. Broadly speaking, their sphere of operations lies in one or more of the following areas: they manage funds for individuals and trusts; they finance foreign trade; they advise industrial companies (there are few major take-overs that get very far before both sides call in a merchant bank); and they are involved in the foreign security business, providing an important link between London and Europe and London and the United States.

The London Stock Exchange is the most important of the eight stock exchanges operating in the British Isles. Members of the Stock Exchange pay an annual fee of £300. There used to be an entrance fee of £1,050 (i.e. one thousand guineas) but this was discontinued in 1975. In addition £1,000 must be paid into the Nomination Redemption Fund when one becomes a member. Until early 1973 a further qualification was that members had to be male, but the restrictions on women becoming members has now been lifted. Members of the Stock Exchange are either stockbrokers, who buy and sell securities on behalf of their clients, or jobbers, who do not deal directly with the public, but with brokers. The jobber makes his living by selling shares at a higher price than he paid for them, an activity which demands a great deal of skill and nerve, but which results in considerable financial benefits for those who possess these attributes, together with a large slice of luck.

Lloyd's is probably best known for its world-wide involvement in maritime insurance. Although this still produces a large amount of revenue, Lloyd's also has interests in many other fields. It is said that it is possible to insure against anything provided that the price is right, and Lloyd's goes a long way towards proving this by providing insurance for statesmen against assassination or serious injury, for farmers against hurricanes and for shipping and air firms against loss of their ships or aircraft. Lloyd's is not a company, but a market for insurance, where individual underwriters transact business. To become an underwriting member of Lloyd's means that one must satisfy rigorous financial requirements, designed to ensure complete business integrity.

While Lloyd's is the best known insurance institution, there are nearly 600 insurance companies in the United Kingdom, with assets of over £22,000 million. As the biggest investors in the country, insurance companies play an important part in Britain's financial life. The most important aspect of insurance is life assurance; it is estimated that 90 per cent of the insurance companies' funds are life funds. Nearly two-thirds of the companies' non-life premiums are earned overseas, with the United States, which accounts for 30 per cent of the total, being the largest single market.

INDUSTRIAL RELATIONS

Trade Unions

Although the origins of the trade union movement are often traced back to the craft guilds of the Middle Ages, the modern trade union is essentially a product of the Industrial Revolution. During the late eighteenth century there were a number of attempts by workers to improve their conditions, and these were usually resisted by the authorities. In 1799 and 1800 Parliament, fearful that the events of the French Revolution might be repeated in Britain, passed the Combination Laws. These Laws, by forbidding working men the right to combine to negotiate for better wages and conditions, effectively checked the growth of unions until 1824, when they were repealed. In 1825, however, a new Act was passed, which once again restricted the right of men to take effective industrial action. During the late twenties and early thirties a number of unions were formed, but were subject to continual harassment.

By the 1840s a number of unions were in existence, usually drawing their membership from those who practised a particular craft. In addition to bargaining with employers these unions were particularly concerned with providing sickness grants and similar benefits for their members. They were still restricted by anti-union legislation, but the first trades union congress which met in 1868 could claim to represent about 118,000 workers. During the next few decades the position of the trade unionist improved, though there were still many battles to be won. In 1900 there were rather more than 2 million workers who were members of 1,323 trade unions. Seventy years later the number of unionists had grown to about 11 million, though as a result of amalgamations the number of unions had fallen to about 480. It is estimated that over 75 per cent of trade unionists belong to the 23 largest unions. In spite of the tendency towards larger unions a large number of British unions are still basically 'craft unions', that is members belong to a union because they have a particular skill, rather than because they belong to a particular industry. This tends to keep the number of unions relatively large, and can also cause demaracation, or 'who does what', disputes. Britain has a labour force of 25.6 million; 22.8 million of these are employees, about half of whom are trade unionists.

The central body of the British trade union movement is the Trades Union Congress (TUC). The Congress itself only meets once a year, when delegates from the member unions meet to discuss matters of concern to the movement. Each year this annual conference elects a General Council, consisting of thirty-four general secretaries of trade unions, and this Council acts as the voice of the TUC for the rest of the year. The only full-time member of the General Council is the General Secretary, who is also the chief officer of the TUC.

There are some 150 trade unions affiliated to the TUC, representing about 10 million workers. Ten large unions account for 6 million workers, two, the Transport and General Workers Union (TGWU) and the Amalgamated Union of Engineering Workers (AUEW), having 3 million members between them.

Since World War II British industry has acquired a reputation for being strike-prone. Britian's record during the sixties, when an average of 5.4 million working days per year were lost through industrial action, compares quite favourably with that of other industrialised countries. Figures for the seventies, however, have been higher. In 1972, the worst year for strikes since the General Strike of 1926, 23.9 million working days were lost. The situation improved in 1973 when the figure was 7.2 million, but deteriorated once more in 1974, when 14.7 million working days were lost, 38 per cent of them being due to the miners' strike early in the year.

Nevertheless it is true that many of Britain's strikes occur within a comparatively small number of industries, for example transport, ship-building and the motor industry, which accentuates the effects. During 1973 almost 50 per cent of strikes lasted only three days. Another feature of British industrial relations is that a large number of stoppages (the Royal Commission of 1968 put the figure as high as 95 per cent) are unofficial (do not have the support of the trade unions).

The Royal Commission appointed in 1965 to investigate the whole field of labour relations recommended the setting up of a Commission on Industrial Relations. This recommendation was put into effect, but as the Commission's role was to bring unions and employers together on a voluntary basis its powers were somewhat limited. Meanwhile the Labour Government was working on a far more controversial measure, details of which were contained in a policy document entitled *In Place of Strife* published early in 1969. The proposals guaranteed the rights of unionists, but also contained measures that the trade unions regarded as totally unacceptable. After a long and bitter struggle within the Labour movement, the TUC announced that it was prepared to give a 'solemn and binding undertaking' to intervene in strikes where unionists were at fault. Although this voluntary declaration fell far short of what the Government was aiming at, the hostility of the unions forced it to back down, and shelve plans for legislation. The Conservative Party, which returned to power in 1970, had no such inhibitions. Shortly after the election the outline of an Industrial Relations Bill was drawn up, and this became law in August 1971. Under the Act unions were required to register with the Registrar of Trade Unions and Employers' Associations. The Act also put the Commission on Industrial Relations on a statutory basis, set up the National Industrial Relations Court, and forbade 'unfair industrial practices' by employers and employees. The TUC felt that the Act restricted its rights and instructed member unions not to register. If a union did not register it would not of course be recognised as official, but the TUC obviously hoped that by adopting a policy of non-co-operation it could render the Act unworkable.

The Act came into effect at the beginning of 1972 and from then until its repeal by a Labour Government in mid-1974 it was a thorn in the flesh of labour relations in Britain. Shortly before the February 1974 election one of the leading spokesmen for the employers commented that the Act was counter-productive as far as relations between unions and management were concerned – a remark which landed him in hot water with some of his colleagues. During 1974 the Labour Government announced that they and the unions had agreed that the future of labour relations in Britain would be decided within the terms of a 'social contract' (see p. 143). However this well-meaning but extremely vague declaration of principle had little effect in a time of unprecedented inflation and economic despondency. In mid-1975 the Government announced that no pay increases were to exceed £6 a week. In September of that year, at the

TUC's annual conference, the trade unions agreed to support the Government's plan by a two to one majority.

The Confederation of British Industry

The Confederation of British Industry (CBI) consists of 13,000 companies and over 200 trade associations and employers' organisations. It provides advisory services to its members and represents the employers in any meetings between the trade unions, management and the Government. In addition it maintains links with similar bodies in other countries.

The Conciliation and Arbitration Service

In September 1974 the Conciliation and Arbitration Service was set up. The Service is an independent body, though it is government-financed, and is designed to intervene in labour disputes at the request of the parties concerned. The board of the Service consists of a chairman and nine other members and has the power to nominate an arbitrator (frequently a leading academic with industrial relations experience) if it feels that such a course is appropriate.

8

Life in Britain Today

POPULATION

At the beginning of the nineteenth century most of the inhabitants of the United Kingdom lived in the country. According to the first official census in 1801, the population of England and Wales was 8.8 million, 7.3 million of whom lived in the countryside. In 1831 agriculture still accounted for the largest sector of the country's labour force, giving work to 28 per cent of all families. By 1851 the population had risen to nearly eighteen million, half of them living in urban areas, London, which had grown in size from just over one million in 1801 to 2.6 million in 1851, was by far the largest city, but industrial centres such as Liverpool, Manchester and Birmingham had also expanded at an unprecedented rate. In 1801 Birmingham had 71,000 inhabitants; 50 years later there were 233,000 people living in the city, while Manchester had grown from 75,000 to 303,000 and Liverpool from 82,000 to 376,000. By the middle of the twentieth century London's population was 8.3 million and Birmingham's 1.1 million, while Manchester and Liverpool had 703,000 and 789,000 inhabitants respectively. It seems that 1951 represented the peak population in the large cities, for at the time of the 1961 census London had 8.1 million inhabitants, while other large cities showed similar small, but nonetheless significant, falls in population.

At the time of the 1971 census the population of the United Kingdom was 55,346,000, 77 per cent of whom lived in urban areas. While it seems unlikely that the population will expand at the rate it did during the nineteenth century in the future, the number of people living in the United Kingdom is still growing steadily each year. It has been estimated that in the year 2003 the population of the United Kingdom will be 59.6 million.

In common with other industrialised countries, Britain has

9

The Mass Media

England's first daily paper, the *Courant*, was published in 1702. During the course of the eighteenth century many more newspapers were founded, including the *Morning Post* in 1772 and *The Times* in 1785. However it was not until the last decade of the nineteenth century that the mass circulation daily paper made its appearance.

In 1896 Alfred Harmsworth (later Lord Northcliffe) founded the *Daily Mail*, and by the beginning of the new century it was selling nearly a million copies a day. The *Mail* was to be the basis of a great newspaper empire that at its height included *The Times*, the *Observer*, the *Daily Mail*, the *Evening News*, the *Daily Mirror* (which, founded in 1903, in 1911 became the first daily paper to top the million mark in circulation) and a number of other weekly and provincial papers and periodicals. In 1900 Arthur Pearson started the *Morning Herald* (later renamed the *Daily Express*) which used techniques similar to those of the *Mail* with equal success.

The rise of the popular press at the end of the nineteenth and the beginning of the twentieth century was the result of a number of factors. Whereas the newspapers of the mid-nineteenth century were directed primarily at the middle and upper classes, the *Daily Mail*, *Daily Express* and *Daily Mirror* were aimed, both in price and content, at the lower-middle and working classes. Using the most up-to-date printing methods, and obtaining a large revenue from advertising. Harmsworth was able to produce the *Daily Mail* more cheaply than its competitors. His distribution arrangements (from 1900 the paper was printed simultaneously in London and Manchester) ensured that he would get nation-wide coverage. Another factor that should be taken into account is that the introduction of compulsory education in 1870 laid the foundations of universal literacy, which undoubtedly contributed to the success of the new papers. The growing political awareness of the working class and their desire to find out 'what was going on' should also be mentioned, though it was not until 1911 that the first socialist paper, the *Daily Herald*, appeared.

During the twentieth century the number of newspaper readers has increased, though paradoxically the number of newspapers has declined. In 1921 there were 12 national morning papers, 21 national Sunday papers and 130 provincial papers (morning or evening). Fifty years later there were 9 national morning papers, 7 national Sunday papers and 86 provincial dailies. In 1921 there were about 1,480 weekly papers; in 1971 the figure had dropped to about 750. It is estimated that in 1920 just under $5\frac{1}{2}$ million newspapers were sold each day; in 1972 the figure was about $22\frac{1}{4}$ million, over 14 million of which were national dailies.

Britain is a relatively small country with good internal communications and it is largely due to this that a national press has developed. It is possible to buy a copy of one of the national papers virtually anywhere in the United Kingdom on the day it is published. National press in practice means London press, because although a number of national papers are printed in Manchester as well as London, all the national papers except one have their headquarters in the capital. The exception is the *Guardian*, founded as the *Manchester Guardian* in 1821, but even this paper now has editorial offices in London. Daily papers outside London are usually published as 'evening' papers and contain a mixture of national and local news. There are, however, a number of regional morning papers, such as the *Yorkshire Post*, the *Western Morning News* and the *Northern Echo*. Scotland has a number of newspapers in addition to those which come from England, the two leading ones being the *Scotsman* published in Edinburgh and the *Glasgow Herald* (Glasgow).

Although many of the leading newspapers have their editorial offices elsewhere, the congested London thoroughfare known as Fleet Street is justifiably regarded as the home of the British press, and over the years this name has become virtually synonymous with the national newspaper industry. One of the interesting characteristics of this industry is that at any one time over half the national newspapers seem in imminent danger of closure. Nor is this impression wholly without foundation, for in recent years a number of papers have ceased publication, both dailies – the *News Chronicle* and the *Daily Sketch*, and Sundays – the *Empire News*, the *Sunday Dispatch*, the *Sunday Citizen* and the *Sunday Graphic*. High circulations do not necessarily guarantee survival. More than two million copies of the *Empire News* were sold each Sunday, while the daily *News Chronicle* had a circulation of over a million.

Virtually every newspaper must supplement the income it receives from sales with revenue from other sources, and the most important of these is advertising. Advertising, however, cannot be entirely divorced from sales figures, as advertisers will only wish to buy space in papers that reach a large number of people. Thus a vicious circle sets in: newspapers with low circulations try to attract advertising to assist their finances and so develop means to improve their sales, but the advertisers are reluctant to use these papers. As circulation declines, so advertisers tend to fall away, which means that revenue continues to decrease. Unless another source of money is found, such as a subsidy, the proprietors will be forced to close down, merge with another paper – which usually amounts to the same thing – or sell to someone who is willing to invest money in a rescue operation. The financial structure of the newspaper industry in Britain is far from simple. In some cases a company will own a large range of papers and magazines, using the dull but solvent titles to support prestigious, but usually impecunious, big names, usually dailies or Sundays. It is by no means uncommon to find that many newspapers are controlled by large commercial groups with diversified interests, and once again the profitable sectors will help to carry the newspapers along. The involvement of large business enterprises in the production of newspapers and the concentration of ownership into a few hands has caused considerable concern in recent years. In 1949 and again in 1962 Royal Commissions were appointed to study this question and also other problems facing the press. In 1974 yet another Royal Commission was set up.

The British national press can be divided roughly into two sections, the 'qualities' or 'heavies', and the 'populars', though such a division is far from absolute. Among the dailies *The Times*, the *Daily Telegraph* and the *Guardian* (plus the specialised *Financial Times*, which concentrates on 'City' news) are considered to be 'qualities'. The *Daily Mirror*, the *Daily Express*, the *Daily Mail* and the *Sun* can be classified as 'popular' papers. The division is made primarily on the basis of how each paper treats the news. The 'qualities' usually have in-depth news items, backed up by articles written by staff writers or outsiders interpreting the news. The 'populars' give space to relatively few news stories, and those that they do cover are often treated superficially. The popular papers also tend to have more photographs than the qualities, and in many cases these are included for their decorative value, rather than their relevance to the news.

Table 1. Circulation of national newspapers (April-September 1975)

DAILIES

The Morning Star	50,000 (approx. figure)
The Financial Times	180,201
The Guardian	314,868
The Times	315,094
The Daily Telegraph	1,323,730
The Daily Mail	1,724,515
The Daily Express	2,798,629
The Sun	3,476,621
The Daily Mirror	3,943,629

SUNDAYS

The Observer	730,832
The Sunday Telegraph	751,858
The Sunday Times	1,347,691
The Sunday Express	3,726,389
The Sunday People	4,184,848
The Sunday Mirror	4,267,025
The News of the World	5,467,089

When one looks at the circulation figures (see Table 1) it is immediately apparent that the sales performance of the populars is decidedly better than that of the qualities. However the qualities not only cost more, they also carry far more of the revenue-earning classified advertising. Over 30 per cent of the *Daily Telegraph*, for example, is made up of pages carrying 'classifieds' (small advertisements closely set in columns under classifications such as 'For Sale', 'Wanted', etc.), compared with about 4 per cent for the *Daily Express* and less than 1 per cent for the *Daily Mirror*. A comparable situation exists with the

Sundays. The qualities, the *Sunday Times*, the *Observer* and the *Sunday Telegraph*, all carry more advertising than editorial matter, a great deal of it in the form of classified advertisements. As in the quality dailies, the emphasis is on giving the background to the news, and all three papers contain articles of considerable length, analysing different aspects of home or foreign events. The popular Sundays, the *News of the World*, the *Sunday People*, the *Sunday Mirror* and the *Sunday Express*, are more concerned with 'human interest' stories and photographs. This formula seems to enjoy quite a lot of success as all four populars have circulations of over four million. Like the qualities they carry advertising, but the emphasis is on display advertisements rather than classifieds.

In addition to carrying news and advertisements the newspapers also have feature articles, reviews, sports pages and financial and business sections, though the proportions devoted to each of these vary considerably from one paper to another. Although some of the Sundays have names resembling those of daily papers, and are indeed owned by the same group, the papers retain their own identities. Thus the *Sunday Express* and the *Daily Express* are both owned by Beaverbrook Newspapers Ltd, but each has its own editor and staff. The same is true of *The Times* and the *Sunday Times*, both part of the Thomson Group, and the *Daily Mirror* and *Sunday Mirror* published by the International Publishing Corporation. Apart from the *Morning Star* which is controlled by the Communist Party, none of the national papers is owned by a political party though this does not mean, of course, that they do not have political opinions. Politically speaking the majority of the British press is inclined to be right of centre. The left-wing *Daily Herald* mentioned earlier changed its name, ownership and outlook during the sixties, rising again as the *Sun*. It is now part of the same group as the *News of the World*.

Something like 4,200 periodicals are published in the United Kingdom, covering a very wide range of topics. The leading serious weeklies are the *New Statesman*, *The Economist* and the *Spectator*, which provide coverage of national and international affairs from different points of the political spectrum. They also have sections dealing with the arts. *Punch* is well known as an old-established humorous weekly, while the irreverent *Private Eye*, founded during the sixties, maintains a somewhat precarious existence sniping at the more pompous features of British life. Women's periodicals such as *Woman* and *Woman's Own* enjoy a wide circulation, as do many of the magazines catering for leisure activities. Although there are a large number of well-illustrated magazines dealing with subjects as varied as gardening, railways, cooking, architecture and attractive girls, Britain has no illustrated news magazines of the *Paris-Match* or *Stern* type. *Picture Post*, which enjoyed great popularity during the forties, was unable to survive the competition of television, while attempts to launch new magazines of this type have proved unsuccessful.

RADIO AND TELEVISION

The first commercial broadcasting to be carried out in Britain was when the Marconi Company was given permission to transmit for one hour a day from radio station 2 LO. In December 1922 Mr John Reith (later Lord Reith) was appointed General Manager of the British Broadcasting Company, and in 1927 he became Director-General of the new British Broadcasting Corporation. Reith was to have a great effect on how the BBC carried out its duties. In his opinion it was the BBC's responsibility to give the public, not what they wanted, but what 'they ought to want'. As the BBC was in a monopoly position this in practice meant that the public had to accept what the Corporation and its Director-General thought was good for them. Reith was also very concerned that the BBC should retain its independence of the government and commercial interests. Before long the Corporation built up a considerable reputation for impartiality in its news reports, and this was enhanced during the Second World War by the radio reports beamed to occupied Europe.

Until the 1950s the BBC had a monopoly of broadcasting in Britain, but with the advent of television there was considerable pressure from commercial interests to establish other firms with permits to broadcast. Largely owing to the tactics of a small but extremely well-organised pressure group, the commercial lobby won the day, and in March 1954 the Bill to establish an 'independent' television authority was passed. Fourteen months later the first programmes containing advertising spots were broadcast.

At the present time the BBC controls two national television services, four national radio services and nineteen local radio stations. The Independent Broadcasting Authority (originally the Independent Television Authority) controls the activities of the commercial television companies and also the radio companies that have recently been formed. The BBC has a board of governors who, under their chairman, are responsible for supervising the programmes that are transmitted. These governors are appointed by the Crown, on the advice of the Government. The day-to-day running of the BBC is in the hands of the Director-General, who is chosen by the board of governors. The BBC is financed by a grant from Parliament, which is derived from the revenue received from the sale of television licences. The BBC also gets revenue from selling programmes to overseas television companies, and from the sale of books, magazines and other publications, including the *Radio Times*. The BBC's external services also receive government support.

The Independent Broadcasting Authority consists of a chairman and ten other members appointed by the Minister of Posts and Telecommunications. The IBA does not produce programmes itself, but issues licences to, and supervises, the transmitting companies. There are fifteen programme companies, for example Thames (London), Granada (North West) and Anglia (East Anglia), that hold contracts to provide programmes for the fourteen regions into which Britain is divided. (London has two companies, of which one provides programmes during the week, the other at weekends.) The IBA is financed by rental received from programme companies for use of transmitting facilities. Every six years the contracts granted to programme companies are reviewed; each company has to apply for a renewal of its licence, while new companies are invited to apply at the same time. The programme companies receive nothing from licence fees, and are entirely dependent on the money they get from advertising. In 1972 the Sound Broadcasting Act was passed, ending the BBC's monopoly of radio broadcasting. It is envisaged that there will eventually be a network of up to sixty local stations operating on a commercial basis. Some of the strongest criticism of commercial radio on a local basis has come from local and regional newspapers, and it is interesting to note that an effort has been made to give newspapers a share in the ownership of the stations. At the same time measures have been taken to ensure that control of the media is not concentrated into too few hands. The local newspapers' objection to local commercial radio was largely due to the fear that the radio stations would take away the advertising that provides the newspapers with a great deal of their revenue.

Television viewing is the most popular leisure activity in Britain. It is estimated that over 90 per cent of the population have television sets in their homes. A large proportion of the programmes shown are produced in Britain, though there are a number of American series on both BBC and ITV. A few programmes come from other countries, Australia, for example, but very few foreign language productions reach the screen as the British seem to object to sub-titles.

The range of programmes shown varies considerably in quality. There are a number of current affairs, educational, sport, and cultural programmes and a wide selection of plays, series, films and variety shows. Owing to the competition that exists between BBC and ITV there is often a tendency for similar programmes to be broadcast at the same time, for example, one channel may be producing a variety show, which leads to the other channel having a variety show at the same time, with what it considers to be bigger and better stars.

In 1964 the BBC was granted a second television channel, BBC 2, giving it what ITV regarded as an unfair advantage. It was the intention of the BBC that programmes on BBC 2 would include a high proportion of minority interest programmes, and although this happens in some cases (for example the Open University programmes are transmitted on BBC 2) there is evidence that at peak viewing times the battle of the ratings once again becomes of key importance (the ratings show how many people watch each programme). At the beginning of the seventies the ITV companies had high hopes of getting a second channel too, but after some discussion the government decided not to give the fourth channel the go-ahead.

Opinions about the standard of programmes shown on British television differ widely. It is probably true to say that some of the news and current affairs reporting is of a very high standard, while there are also excellent drama productions which enable many people to see plays they would not be able to see in the theatre. On a number of occasions there have been attempts by self-appointed protectors of public morals to influence the kind of programmes broadcast on television, but there seems little evidence that the British public is exposing itself to great moral danger by sitting in front of the television screen for some fifteen hours a week (the average viewing time per head of population).

10

Religious Life

Christianity came to Britain in Roman times though its influence declined after the withdrawal of the legions early in the fifth century. In 596 Pope Gregory sent a party of monks led by Augustine to convert the English and it was these men and their successors who established the position of the Roman Catholic Church in the country. Throughout the Middle Ages the English kings acknowledged at least nominal allegiance to Rome, but by the sixteenth century it was clear that relations were becoming somewhat strained. In 1534 Henry VIII broke with Rome, the immediate cause of the breach being the Pope's refusal to recognise his divorce from Catherine of Aragon. Although his elder daughter, Mary Tudor, tried to re-establish the Roman Catholic Church in England during her reign (1553–8), she was unsuccessful. Her sister Elizabeth had been brought up a Protestant and the Settlement made soon after she came to the throne confirmed the position of the Protestant Church of England. The Elizabethan Church Settlement, however, did not end religious controversy in Britain, as even the most cursory glance at the history books will show. Matters of faith were rarely far from the minds of those involved in the conflicts of the seventeenth century, though once again the Church of England triumphed when the Protestant William III replaced the Catholic James II on the throne in 1688. Throughout the eighteenth century Nonconformists and Roman Catholics were barred from holding public office, but the 1828 Test Act and the 1829 Catholic Emancipation Act lifted many of the restrictions laid upon those who were not members of the Anglican Church.

THE CHURCH OF ENGLAND

The Church of England is still the established Church in England. (In Wales the Church of England was disestablished in 1920, largely because the Welsh have a strong Nonconformist tradition.) The head of the Church of England is the monarch and part of the coronation ceremony includes an oath in which the monarch promises to protect the position of the Anglican Church. Archbishops, bishops and deans are appointed by the Crown, though in fact the advice of the Prime Minister is the decisive factor. The involvement of the Prime Minister is interesting because although the monarch must be a member of the Church of England by law the Prime Minister need not be a member of the Anglican or indeed any other Church. (It seems likely that this method of appointing senior members of the Church will be changed in the near future.)

The links between Church and state can also be seen in the fact that archbishops and twenty-four other bishops sit in the House of Lords and participate in debates on equal terms with members of the peerage. Unlike other members of the Upper House, however, they do not sit for life, giving up their seats when they retire from their sees. The Church of England must obtain parliamentary approval if it wishes to change its form of worship, and this approval is by no means always forthcoming. In 1929 the Church Assembly produced a revised prayer book, which was accepted by the House of Lords, but rejected by the Commons. As the Church as a whole was in favour of the new prayer book, the action of the Commons raised the whole question of the position of the state Church, and there were those who suggested that disestablishment was the answer. The question of disestablishment has also come up more recently. In 1970 a commission set up to consider the relationship between Church and state recommended that the status of the Church of England should be maintained, but that a number of changes should be introduced to give the Church more autonomy. The most important of these proposals were that the Church should have final authority over its forms of doctrine and worship, so avoiding a repetition of the 1929 situation; that the methods of selecting bishops should be revised; that all ministers of religion should be able to stand for Parliament; and that leading members of other churches should be invited to sit in the House of Lords, alongside the senior bishops of the Church of England. Some people felt that the commission did not go far enough, and should have recommended a complete break between Church and state, while others felt that the changes proposed were too radical to be acceptable.

England is divided into two provinces, Canterbury and York, and forty-three dioceses, twenty-nine of which are in the Province of Canterbury, while the remaining fourteen come under the authority of the Archbishop of York. Although the Archbishop of Canterbury and the Archbishop of York are nominally of equal status, in practice the former, who is styled 'Primate of All England', is the senior, and is in fact the professional head of the Anglican Church. Many of the bishoprics are of considerable antiquity; Canterbury was first established at the end of the sixth century by St Augustine, while others, such as Leicester, set up in 1926, and Guildford (1927) were founded to meet the needs of present centres of population. In the older dioceses the bishop has his seat in an ancient cathedral. Most of these cathedrals were built during the Middle Ages and they embody a fascinating variety of styles, sometimes providing an outline of several centuries of English architecture in one building. The majority of the medieval cathedrals are extremely impressive buildings, even more so when one takes into account the relatively primitive technology of those responsible for designing and erecting them. In the case of dioceses of more recent foundation the cathedral is usually a large parish church adapted to suit the responsibilities of its new status, examples being Leicester, Manchester and Derby. In some dioceses, however, notably Truro, Liverpool, Guildford and Coventry, new cathedrals have been built in the last hundred years or so.

There are about 14,300 ecclesiastical parishes in England, each centred on a parish church, Most parishes have a resident parish priest, while a large town parish will probably also have one or more assistant priests or curates. In early Christian times the founder of a parish had the privilege of appointing the parish priest, this right of patronage being known as the advowson. During the Middle Ages many advowsons were in the possession of monasteries, and when these were dissolved by Henry VIII the advowsons passed into the hands of the Crown, or lay landowners who had bought monastic land. Today patronage is exercised by bishops and archbishops, cathedral chapters, the Crown, lay landowners – including some large companies – the universities, particularly Oxford and Cambridge colleges, and trusts. In February 1975 the General Synod of the Church voted to end the old system of patronage and to give the Church more control. Most livings are supported by endowments and sometimes by land known as a glebe. Other sources of income are fees for services such as marriages and funerals, while the parish priest is also entitled to the proceeds of the Easter Collection. Incumbents of livings where the endowment is insufficient may receive assistance from central funds of the Church or a stewardship scheme arranged by parishioners.

The Church of England does not have a formal register of members. One becomes a member of the Church on baptism, and this membership is often re-endorsed at confirmation, usually at the age of fourteen or so. An electoral roll, consisting of parishioners over the age of sixteen, is compiled every year, usually at the Easter communion. However having one's name on the electoral role is not necessarily proof of active Church membership, nor does it impose any compulsory duties such as payment of a church tax. In these circumstances it is not surprising that any accurate measurement of membership of the Church of England is virtually impossible. It has been estimated that over 27 million of the population of England have been baptised into the Church, almost 10 million have been confirmed, while 2.5 million appear on the electoral rolls. The appearance of a name on the roll does not necessarily mean that the elector plays an active part in parish activities by taking advantage of his right to vote for parish officials, or standing for election himself. Church attendance is also difficult to estimate, though few would dispute that Church of England congregations, like those of the other churches, have declined during the present century.

Although the Church of England is the state Church it receives no financial assistance from the government, apart from salaries paid to chaplains in the armed forces and money provided for church schools. The main financial support for the Church comes from the free-will offerings of Church members and from its own land and capital. Although the amount of land held by the Church has shrunk from its heyday just before the Reformation, the Church of England is still the third largest landowner in the country, after the Forestry Commission and the Crown. The assets of the Church, estimated at over £420 million, are administered by the Church Commissioners, and it is these gentlemen who by wise investment on the Stock Exchange have managed to increase the income of the Church by a considerable amount in recent years. Nevertheless there are many demands on the resources of the Church, including salaries, the upkeep of ancient churches and cathedrals and the financing of various services provided by the Church at home and overseas.

Between 1919 and 1970 the governing body of the Church of England was the Church Assembly, but in September 1970 elections were held for the new General Synod of the Church. The General Synod, which is composed of the bishops, and representatives of the clergy and laity, has spiritual, legislative and administrative functions. At the local level there are deanery diocesan synods, which are responsible for involving the individual parishes in the life of the Church. Important issues must be discussed in the diocesan synods before being submitted to the General Synod for a final decision.

In addition to the Church of England in England, the Anglican Communion extends to other parts of the British Isles and throughout the world. The (unestablished) Church of Wales is headed by the Archbishop of Wales, and there are also the Episcopal Church in Scotland and the rather misleadingly named Church of Ireland, which covers both Northern Ireland and the Irish Republic. Every tenth year the Lambeth Conference (Lambeth Palace is the London residence of the Archbishop of Canterbury) meets, and is attended by Anglican bishops from all over the world. The Conference has no executive authority, but provides a useful forum for the exchange of ideas.

THE CHURCH OF SCOTLAND

The Church of Scotland took its Presbyterian form after the Reformation, and maintained its opposition to episcopacy (rule by bishops) throughout the seventeenth century, in spite of Charles I's attempts to remodel it on the lines of the Church of England. The status of the Church of Scotland was confirmed by the Treaty of Union between England and Scotland in 1707. The Church of Scotland, which has the sovereign in her capacity as Queen of Scotland at its head, is completely free from parliamentary control. All ministers of the Church are of equal status, though each year a Moderator is elected to preside over the meeting of the General Assembly, which consists of elected ministers and elders of the Kirk. Each of the 2,000 or so churches are under the local control of the Kirk Session (the ministers and elders of the church), while above this is the Court of the Presbytery, the Court of Synod and the General Assembly.

THE ROMAN CATHOLIC CHURCH

After the Reformation the Roman Catholic Church in England suffered considerable hardships. By the nineteenth century, however, attitudes had mellowed somewhat and the hierarchy was reintroduced to England in 1850 and to Scotland in 1878. At the present time there are seven Roman Catholic provinces, twenty episcopal dioceses and some 2,400 parishes. The head of the Roman Catholic Church in England is the Archbishop of Westminster. It is estimated that the Roman Catholic Church has about six million members in Britain, the majority of whom live in large towns.

Recently there have been many discussions between the Roman Catholic Church and members of other churches in Britain, as elsewhere in the world, on the subject of co-operation; and a number of interdenominational services have been held. The age-old distrust between Protestants and Catholics seems to have died down in most parts of Britain, though the past, or a highly-coloured version of the past, is still remembered in Scotland, while the tragedy of Northern Ireland shows that for some the past and present are inextricably linked.

THE FREE CHURCHES

The Methodist Church, which today has some 651,000 members, was founded by a Church of England clergyman called John Wesley. At first Wesley tried to maintain his links with the Anglican Church, but the opposition of the hierarchy of that institution to his methods and his doctrine forced him to break away in 1784 and ordain his own clergy. A number of divisions occurred within the Methodist Church during the nineteenth century, but most of the schisms were healed in 1932. In the sixties and again in 1972 an attempt was made to bring together the Methodist and Anglican Churches. Although the proposal was accepted by the Methodists, it failed to get the necessary majority from the Anglicans, and so the idea came to nothing. Individual Methodist churches have a considerable degree of self-government, and each year a conference, which is chaired by an elected president is held to discuss matters of concern to the church.

In 1972 the oldest community of dissenters in Britain, the Congregationalists, united with the English Presbyterian Church to form the United Reformed Church. Other Christian groups represented in Britain include the Baptists, who have about 2,000 churches, the Society of Friends (Quakers), first active in the mid-seventeenth century, the Salvation Army, founded by William Booth in 1865, and the Unitarian Church.

The Jewish community in Britain is divided into two groups, the Orthodox, consisting of about 90 per cent of practising Jews, and the Reform, which originated during the last century. The leading member of the Jewish community is the Chief Rabbi, who belongs to the Orthodox group. The Jewish community numbers about 410,000, and it has 240 synagogues, mainly in urban areas. Other non-Christian religions include Muslims and Buddhists. Most of the adherents of these religions come from the ranks of the Commonwealth immigrants who have settled in Britain since the Second World War.

Glossary

(The purpose of this glossary is to give the meaning of certain expressions and terms in the context in which they are used in the text. The meaning given here is not necessarily the only one.)

Abdication Renunciation of rights to throne by sovereign. The most recent abdication was that of Edward VIII (the late Duke of Windsor) in 1936.

Act Statute passed by both Houses of Parliament and given the Royal Assent.

Adjournment Postponement of proceedings (e.g. in Parliament) until another occasion.

Adoption meeting Meeting at which a parliamentary candidate is chosen.

Anglican Of the Church of England.

Appeal (legal) To take a case to a higher court.

Audience (of royalty) Interview with or presentation to the sovereign.

Back bencher Member of Parliament who is not a member of the government (i.e. is not of ministerial rank) or the Shadow Cabinet.

Back-to-back houses Houses with a common rear wall and no rear access (usually built in the late eighteenth or early nineteenth century).

Bail (legal) Temporary release from custody on a security to appear for trial; also the security.

Ballot Secret vote (introduced in British elections in 1872); *ballot paper* paper on which the vote is recorded; *ballot box* box in which the paper is inserted after the vote has been recorded.

Bank holiday Public holiday in England and Wales, e.g. Boxing Day (the day after Christmas), the Spring Bank Holiday.

Bar (legal) Barristers collectively, or profession of barrister (barristers are 'called to the Bar' when they qualify).

Bench Collective term for magistrates or judges when presiding in court.

Bill (political) Draft of an Act of Parliament submitted to Parliament for debate.

Black Rod Gentleman Usher of the Black Rod (so called because he carries a black rod or stick), usher of the Lord Chamberlain's department of the royal household, also usher of the House of Lords.

Building society Financial institution to which members lend money at a certain rate of interest and which in turn lends money for the purchase of property – usually houses.

By-election Election in a single constituency during the life of Parliament following death or retirement of an MP.

Canvass To try to obtain support for a candidate at an election by interviewing individual voters.

Census Official counting of the population; in Great Britain a census has been taken every ten years since 1801.

Chief constable Chief officer in police force outside London (in the Metropolitan Police District – roughly Greater London – and the City of London the chief officers are Commissioners of Police).

Circuit District through which a judge travels when attending courts.

City (The) City of London, particularly when referring to financial institutions such as Stock Exchange, banks, insurance companies, etc.

Civil List Sum voted by Parliament for household and personal expenses of sovereign.

Civil servant Salaried government official.

Civil War War (1642–6) between Parliament and King Charles I. The king was defeated and was executed in 1649.

Classifieds Small advertisements appearing in columns of newspapers or journals classified under headings such as 'For Sale', 'Situations Vacant' (jobs), etc.

Coalition Combination of two or more political parties to form a Government (or Opposition).

Constituency Body of voters – in parliamentary terms, area for which an MP is elected and which he represents in Parliament.

Council house House built and maintained by a local authority (i.e. a council) and rented to tenants.

'Daily' (paper) Newspaper that appears six days a week (cf. 'Sunday').

Diocese Area under the authority of a bishop.

Disestablish (ecclesiastical) To withdraw state support and patronage from Church.

Display advertisement Advertisement that is spread over a portion of a page of a newspaper or journal (cf. 'classified').

Dissolution (of Parliament) Bringing a session of Parliament to an end.

Division Separation of Parliament into two for counting votes.

Ecclesiastical Relating to the Church or to clergymen.

Electorate (parliamentary) People over eighteen years of age who are entitled to vote in a parliamentary election.

Equity (legal) System of law existing alongside statute law and common law which supersedes them when they conflict.

Fabian Society Socialist society formed in 1884 to introduce socialism gradually through parliamentary means. Has tended to attract intellectuals; famous Fabians include Bernard Shaw, H. G. Wells, G. K. Chesterton and many past and present Labour Party ministers.

Filibuster To prolong debate on a Bill so that its passage through Parliament cannot be completed in the time available. (An American term.)

Flat racing (the flat) Horse racing over level ground without hedges or ditches.

Fleet Street Street in London where there are a large number of national (and provincial) newspaper offices.

Friendly Society Association whose members pay contributions to insure financial help in sickness or old age.

Front bencher Member of the Government or senior member of Opposition (usually in Cabinet or Shadow Cabinet).

Graduate Person who holds a university degree.

Honour Title or award granted by the sovereign (almost always on ministerial advice). Honours are traditionally awarded twice a year, at New Year, and on the sovereign's official birthday. They can be given on other occasions, e.g. dissolution of Parliament.

Immigrant Usually in context 'Commonwealth immigrant' referring to person originally coming from 'new' Commonwealth, West Indies, Pakistan (which is no longer a Commonwealth member), India, Bangladesh, etc.

Incumbent (ecclesiastical) Clergyman holding a living (as priest).

Independent (political) Politician who belongs to no political party or group.

Jacobite Supporter of the Stuart line and of the descendants of James II who abdicated in 1688.

Junior (legal) Barrister who assists senior counsel (barrister) in presentation of a case in court.

Kirk The Church of Scotland as distinct from the Church of England (kirk: Scottish form of 'church').

Living (ecclesiastical) Benefice, i.e. in Church of England, income-producing property supporting a priest.

Lobby (political) In sense of division lobbies, two chambers into which MPs go when they vote, one for 'Ayes' and one for 'Noes'. Also place where MPs meet constituents, journalists, etc. (hence 'lobby correspondents', journalists particularly concerned with politics).

Lord Chamberlain A prominent official of the Royal Household.

Lord Protector Title held by Oliver Cromwell as head of state 1653–8, and briefly by his son Richard.

Maisonette Small house, or completely self-contained part of large house used as dwelling.

Marginal seat (political) Constituency where the majority of the sitting member is low, which means the seat might be won by a rival party at an election (cf. 'safe seat').

Middle Ages Historical period from (roughly) AD 1000 to *c*.1450.

Minister (political) Person controlling or administering department of state. The most powerful minister is the Prime Minister, also known as the First Lord of the Treasury. Other key ministers are the Chancellor of the Exchequer (finance minister), Home Secretary (Secretary of State for Home Affairs), Foreign Secretary and Lord Chancellor. Large 'departments' are headed by Secretaries of State, e.g. Secretary of State for Defence, Secretary of State for Health and Social Security. In the departments there may be junior ministers, e.g. Minister for Transport Industries within the Department of the Environment, and Ministers of State. Junior ministers are known either as Parliamentary Secretaries or Parliamentary Under-Secretaries of State, depending on the status of the minister in charge of the department.

Ministry (political) A government department, e.g. Department of the Environment, Ministry of Defence. Administered by a politician (see above) and staffed by civil servants.

Mortgage Money loan advanced by building society, council, etc. for purchase of dwelling or other property, with the house etc. being used as security.

Nationalisation Taking over of business concerns by the state.

Nonconformist Person who does not accept the doctrines of an established church, especially Church of England, usually excluding Roman Catholics.

Open University Institution (first students accepted 1971) which provides university-level courses in students' homes by means of television and radio lectures and correspondence courses.

Oxbridge Oxford and Cambridge Universities, i.e. the ancient universities.

Point-to-point Cross-country race for horses.

Polytechnic Institution of higher education financed and controlled by local authorities.

Post-graduate student studying for a higher degree, (e.g. MA, Master of Arts, PhD, Doctor of Philosophy) or diploma.

Precedent (legal) Previous decision or action which provides an authoritative rule for similar cases.

Presbyterian Church Church governed by a council or assembly of 'elders' or officials, especially the Church of Scotland.

Provinces England outside London (hence 'provincial').

Puisne judge (legal) Judge in a superior court of rank lower than chief justice.

Question Time Period during parliamentary day set aside for MPs to question ministers.

Rates Local property tax.

Referendum Direct vote by citizens on a political issue.

Returning officer Official responsible for arranging and conducting an election.

Safe seat (political) Constituency where the sitting member has a large majority and there is little or no danger of any rival poiltical party winning the seat at an election (cf. 'marginal seat').

Sandwich course Course (especially at polytechnics and technical colleges) where students spend alternate periods of time at work and studying at the institution.

Semi-detached house House that has one common wall with another house.

Session (political) Period for which Parliament sits.

Shadow Cabinet Group composed of the leader of the Opposition and his or her senior colleagues in Parliament.

Sheriff Official representing the Crown in counties with various ceremonial, judicial and electoral functions.

'Stand for Parliament' Attempt to get elected to Parliament by being nominated at an election (cf. American expression 'run for office').

Steeplechasing Horse racing over hedges and ditches.

Suffrage (political) The right to vote.

'Sunday' Newspaper published on Sundays.

Synod Assembly of clergy (and lay representatives) for discussing and deciding ecclesiastical affairs.

The Tower (of London) Fortress and royal palace traditionally used as place of imprisonment and execution for offenders against the state – now a museum, though still garrisoned.

Tudor period The Tudors came to power in 1485 when Henry Tudor (later Henry VII) defeated Richard III. The fifth and last Tudor monarch, Elizabeth I, died in 1603.

Undergraduate Student studying for first degree.

Underwriter Person who carries on an insurance business.

Verdict (legal) Decision of jury as to whether the accused in a trial is guilty or not guilty.

Westminster Parliament.

Whitehall Area of London where the most important ministries are found, e.g. the Treasury, Home Office, Foreign Office.

Whip (political) (a) Party official responsible for maintaining party discipline; (b) Letter setting out instructions for attendances at debates sent to MPs by the Whips' office.

Workhouse Institution, especially in nineteenth-century Britain, where those unable to support themselves were given food, shelter and work, all of a low standard (see novels of e.g. Dickens and Hardy).

Writ Written command from sovereign, court, etc. requiring some specific action, e.g. writ for an election.

Select Bibliography

GENERAL

Central Office of Information, *Britain: An official handbook*, HMSO
(Her Majesty's Stationery Office), Annual
Central Statistical Office, *Annual Abstract of Statistics*, HMSO, Annual
Sampson, A., *A New Anatomy of Britain*, Hodder & Stoughton, 1971.
(See also *Anatomy of Britain*, 1962, by the same author)
Whitaker's Almanac, J. Whitaker & Sons, Annual

HISTORICAL AND GEOGRAPHICAL BACKGROUND

Fleure, H. J., *A Natural History of Man in Britain*, Collins Fontana, 1971
Gregg, P., *A Social and Economic History of Britain 1760–1947*, Harrap,
1971
Marwick, A., *Britain in the Century of Total War*, Bodley Head, 1968/
Penguin, 1970
Stamp, L. Dudley and Beaver, S. H., *The British Isles: A geographic and
economic survey*, Longman, 1971
Taylor, A. J. P., *England 1914–1945*, Oxford University Press, 1965/
Penguin 1970
Thomson, D., *England in the Nineteenth Century*, Penguin, 1970
Thomson, D., *England in the Twentieth Century*, Penguin, 1970
Trueman, A. E., *Geology and Scenery in England and Wales*, Penguin, 1971

GOVERNMENT AND POLITICS

Birch, A. H., *The British System of Government*, George Allen & Unwin,
1970
Blake, R., *The Conservative Party from Peel to Churchill*, Eyre & Spottis-
woode, 1970
Blondel, J., *Voters, Parties and Leaders*, Penguin, 1969
Butler, D., and Freeman, J., *British Political Facts 1900–68*, Macmillan,
1969
Butler, D., and Kavanagh, D., *The British General Election of October
1974*, Macmillan, 1975. (D. Butler has also been involved with books
written on every general election since the Second World War – usually
as senior author)
Butler, D. and Stokes, D., *Political Change in Britain*, Macmillan 1969/
Penguin 1971
Hanson, A. and Crick, B., *The House of Commons in Transition*, Fontana,
1970

Jennings, I., *The Queen's Government*, Penguin, 1967
King, A., *British Members of Parliament: A Self-Portrait*, Macmillan, 1974
Mackenzie, K. R., *The English Parliament*, Penguin, 1965
McKenzie, R. T., *British Political Parties*, Heinemann, 1964
Mackintosh, J. P., *The British Cabinet*, Stevens Methuen, 1968
Pelling, H., *A Short History of the Labour Party*, Macmillan, 1972
Rose, R., *Politics in England Today*, Faber, 1974
The Times Guide to the House of Commons, October 1974, The Times, 1974

LOCAL GOVERNMENT

Redcliffe-Maud, Lord, and Wood, B., *English Local Government Reformed*, 1974, Oxford University Press
Richards, P., *The Reformed Local Government System*, George Allen & Unwin, 1973

THE MONARCHY

Duncan, A., *The Reality of Monarchy*, Heinemann 1970/Pan 1973
Hamilton, W., *My Queen and I*, Quartet, 1975
Martin, K., *The Crown and the Establishment*, Hutchinson 1962/Penguin 1963

THE LEGAL SYSTEM

Brown, J., and Howes, G. (eds.), *The Police and the Community*, Saxon House, 1975
Harding, A., *A Social History of English Law*, Penguin, 1966
Street, H., *Freedom, the Individual and the Law*, Penguin, 1972
Whitaker, B., *The Police*, Eyre & Spottiswoode/Penguin, 1964

THE WELFARE STATE

Bruce, M., *The Coming of the Welfare State*, Batsford, 1971
Lynes, T., *The Penguin Guide to Supplementary Benefits*, Penguin, 1974
New Society, a weekly magazine containing articles dealing with many aspects of the welfare state and related topics. Sleeman, J., *The Welfare State*, George Allen & Unwin, 1973
Titmuss, R., *Essays on the Welfare State*, George Allen & Unwin, 1963
Willmott, P., *Consumer's Guide to the British Social Services*, Penguin, 1975

EDUCATION

Benn, C., and Simon, B., *Half-way there*, Penguin, 1972
Burgess, T., *A Guide to English Schools*, Penguin, 1969
Douglas, J., *The Home and the School*, MacGibbon & Kee, 1964/Panther 1969
Douglas, J., Ross, J., and Simpson, H., *All Our Future*, Peter Davies 1968/Panther 1971

Green, V., *The Universities*, Penguin, 1969
Lawson, J., and Silver, H., *A Social History of Education in England*, Methuen, 1973
Robinson, E., *The New Polytechnics*, Penguin, 1968
Smith, W. O. Lester, *Education in Great Britain*, Oxford University Press, 1968
Tunstall, J. (ed.), *The Open University Opens*, Routledge and Kegan Paul, 1974

INDUSTRY AND COMMERCE

Bacon, R., and Ellis, W., *Britain's Economic Problem*, Macmillan, 1976
Brittain, S., *Steering the Economy: the role of the Treasury*, Secker & Warburg 1969/Penguin 1971
Cairncross, A., *Britain's Economic Prospects Reconsidered*, George Allen & Unwin, 1971
Caves, R. and associates, *Britain's Economic Prospects*, The Brookings Institute/George Allen & Unwin 1968
Clarke, W., *The City in the World Economy*, Penguin, 1967
Clayton, G., *British Insurance*, Elek, 1971
Clegg, H., *The System of Industrial Relations in Great Britain*, Blackwell, 1970
Donaldson, P., *Guide to the British Economy*, Penguin, 1970
Ferris, P., *The City*, Gollancz, 1960/Penguin 1965
Hooberman, B., *An Introduction to British Trade Unions*, Penguin, 1974
McRae, H., and Cairncross, F., *Capital City: London as a financial centre*, Eyre Methuen, 1973
Morgan, E., and Thomas, W., *The Stock Exchange: its history and functions*, Elek 1972
Pelling, H., *A History of British Trade Unionism*, Macmillan, 1972/Penguin, 1970
Pringle, R., *Banking in Britain*, Methuen, 1975
Revell, J., *The British Financial System*, Macmillan, 1973
Turner, G., *Business in Britain*, Eyre & Spottiswoode, 1969

LIFE IN BRITAIN

Booker, C., *The Neophiliacs*, Collins 1969/Fontana 1970
Fletcher, R., *The Family and Marriage in Britain*, Penguin, 1969
Gorer, G., *Sex and marriage in England Today*, Nelson, 1971
Office of Population Censuses and Surveys, *The General Household Survey*, HMSO, 1973
Hiro, D., *Black British, White British*, Eyre & Spottiswoode 1971/Penguin 1973
Hoggart, R., *The Uses of Literacy*, Chatto & Windus, 1957/Penguin 1969
Ryder, J. and Silver, H., *Modern English Society 1850–1970*, Methuen, 1970
Young, M. and Willmott, P., *The Symmetrical Family*, Routledge and Kegan Paul, 1973
Young, M., and Willmott, P., *Family and Kinship in East London*, Routledge & Kegan Paul, 1967/Penguin, 1969

PRESS AND BROADCASTING

Briggs, A., *The History of Broadcasting in the United Kingdom:* Vol. I
　The Birth of Broadcasting, 1961; Vol. II The Golden Age of Wireless,
　1965; Vol. III The War of Words, 1970; all published by Oxford
　University Press
Williams, R., *Communications*, Chatto & Windus 1966/Penguin 1970

Index